A Spiritual Look at the Human-Pet Bond

Pet Loss: A Spiritual Guide is a practical handbook which analyzes the emotional and psychological responses to pet death grief. The clear explanations and self-help format provide comfort and assistance for the bereaved.

This book gives you useful answers to your questions regarding final arrangements, from cremation to burial options. Moreover, never before has a book on pet loss dealt with the spiritual perspective of the human-pet bond. Eleanor Harris guides you through healing meditations and cermonies to assist you in reuniting with your pet on a spiritual level.

Pet Loss: A Spiritual Guide isn't limited to pet death. It confronts all types of pet loss, including the stolen pet, the pet given up for adoption, and the runaway pet. Harris' compassion does not end here—she's even included a section on how to console your child during the loss.

This book will help you bid farewell, give blessings, and assist your deceased pet to the spiritual plane.

Pet Loss

A Spiritual Guide

✦

About the Author

Eleanor Harris is a philosopher and a pagan of diversified spiritual and magical practice. She is a writer who aspires to educate society about pagan spiritual and magical practice as well as pet bereavement and communication. Her freelance writing concerning animal rights issues has been published in New Jersey newspaper editorials. She has worked at a pet cemetery and held a seat on the board of directors for The Pet Adoption League, one of New Jersey's largest pet welfare organizations.

Eleanor is an author of *The Crafting and Use of Ritual Tools* and has an upcoming book tentatively titled *Book of Power: Ancient Egyptian Magic*.

To Write to the Author

If you wish to contact the author or would like more information about this book, please write to the author in care of Llewellyn Worldwide and we will forward your request. Both the author and publisher appreciate hearing from you and learning of your enjoyment of this book and how it has helped you. Llewellyn Worldwide cannot guarantee that every letter written to the author can be answered, but all will be forwarded. Please write to:

Eleanor L. Harris
c/o Llewellyn Worldwide
P.O. Box 64383-K-347-6, St. Paul, MN 55164-0383,
U.S.A.

Please enclose a self-addressed, stamped envelope or $1.00 to cover costs. If outside the U.S.A., enclose an international postal reply coupon.

Pet Loss

A Spiritual Guide

Eleanor L. Harris

1998
Llewellyn Publications
St. Paul, Minnesota 55164–0383, U.S.A.

First Edition
Second Printing, 1998

Cover design: Maria Mazzara
Cover photo: PhotoDisc Inc. © 1995
Interior art: Carrie Westfall
Book design and layout: Connie Hill
Editor: Rosemary Wallner
Project Coordinator: Connie Hill

Library of Congress Cataloging-in-Publication Data
    Harris, Eleanor L., 1970–
        Pet loss : a spiritual guide / Eleanor L. Harris
            p.   cm.
        Includes bibliographical references.
        ISBN 1–56718–347–6 (pbk.)
            1. Pet owners—Psychology. 2. Pets—Death—
    Psychological aspects. 3. Bereavement —Psychological
    aspects. 4. Funeral rites and ceremonies. 5. Pet owners—
    Religious life. I. Title.
    SF411.47.H37   1997
    155.9'37—dc21   96-47971
                                                    CIP

Printed in the U.S.A.

Llewellyn Publications
A Division of Llewellyn Worldwide, Ltd.
P.O. Box K-347-6, St. Paul, MN 55164-038

Dedication

I dedicate this book to my husband, Philip A. Harris, who never ceases to understand and share my work with animals. Philip is a remarkable man who has worked hours of overtime so that we may house and foster animals.

This book is written from my heart to all of you who share the knowing of a beautiful, loving bond between people and their pets.

This book is written in love for the following animals who were a part of our family: Lester and Louis, stray cats; Sasha, a miniature spitz; Cheyenne, 140 pounds of loving Fila; and Birdie, a cockatiel who stole my heart.

Acknowledgments

I would like to thank Dr. Wallace Sife, author of an excellent guidebook focusing on the psychological aspects of pet bereavement, and Abbey Glen Pet Memorial Park and Pleasant Plains Crematorium in Lafayette, New Jersey, for the teachings that furthered my knowledge of both people and their pets.

A special thanks to High Priestess Catherine Ormsby of New Jersey, for a portion of her chakra healing formula found in Chapter 6. You are a cherished friend and teacher.

I thank my parents, Charles and Barbara Lillie, for raising me to love and respect nature and the living creatures that share this world with us. Through their teachings and love of animals, I became so enlightened.

✦

Contents

Introduction

HOW LUCKY WE ARE TO RESIDE ON THIS BEAUTI-
ful earth, surrounded by living creatures, each with their
own unique personality and curious actions. Like people,
animals use their unique traits and behaviors to capture our
interest, wonderment, and love. No action is more reward-
ing than becoming a pet owner to one or more of these
unique creatures. Pet owners place all selfish needs and
actions aside to provide food, shelter, love, and devotion to
a living creature. Oh, how we adore the animals—whether
domestic or wild—as they coax our inner child outward by
their presence. We talk to them, worry about them, and
place their well-being above even our own.

As pagan religious and magical practitioners, we are
dedicated to the preservation, understanding, and care of
the earth and its many wondrous living creatures. It surprised me, however, that our pagan community has not
addressed death more thoroughly. In religions such as

Wicca, rituals bid farewell, give blessings, and assist deceased loved ones to the spiritual plane. Although all pagan religions include lore of Gods and Goddesses who represent the transformation of death and dominate the spiritual realm, little is written on the subject of death—particularly pet death.

Pet loss and pet death are topics gaining attention from the mental health profession. Both are very real and very intense; they are issues that deserve our attention. In this book, you'll find a guide not only to dealing with the emotional responses of a pet's death but also to making final arrangements for your pet. Pagan rituals and meditations are included to help you heal and cope with the loss.

Perhaps you have a pet with whom you have a special, ever-loving relationship or have faced the emotional distress of coping with a beloved pet's death. It is difficult to accept the fact that animals do not live as long as humans. When you've been touched by a pet's devotion and unconditional love, you feel robbed when that pet is suddenly gone from your life. Although you will always remember, cherish, and eternally love your deceased pet, you may face extreme pain over the loss.

Like you, I have experienced the joy of having an animal companion and the grief of pet loss. My fascination with and love of animals has led to times when everything is put aside to house or rescue one. My mother and I adopted stray cats wandering in our neighborhood. I have slammed on the brakes when driving and picked up a dog or cat wandering aimlessly along the road. Caring for and loving my own pets has never been enough; every day I take a few precious moments to assist all animals in need.

My interest in and devotion to animals led to my involvement with the Pet Adoption League, one of the largest animal rescue organizations in New Jersey. I worked day and night to rescue, foster, and preserve the lives of countless abused, neglected, and homeless animals. This experience prompted me to pursue a career as a Pet Grief Counselor at a New Jersey pet cemetery. At the same time, I attended human and pet psychology courses. I studied the human-animal bond and pet bereavement to better equip myself for assisting grieving pet owners. I learned to deal with the phases of grief over the loss of a pet. My studies, however, did not prepare me for the interaction that lay ahead. People react to death in different ways and experiencing these reactions firsthand was a most valuable education.

Being a pagan did not hinder my ability to counsel individuals with different religious beliefs. If anything, it provided a unique perspective that I could share with distressed mourners who were not otherwise religious or who questioned the "taking of their loved one by God." In my counseling, I encountered many religions, philosophies, and personalities. I consoled individuals devoted to a particular religion through the comfort of their beliefs. For others, I used my extensive knowledge of world philosophical and religious beliefs.

Writing this book has been the greatest triumph of my many years of helping both animals and people. I believe it is important for individuals to have a system for coping with loss and obtaining resolution that speaks directly from personal religious beliefs. This only benefits the grieving process and uplifts the breaking heart. I decided, therefore, that it was time our pagan community had a text for coping with the stages of pet loss.

In writing this book, I do not present myself as a professional therapist. I do not consider myself anything more than a human being who understands, recognizes, and feels the bond we share with our animal friends.

Chapter One

The Human & Pet Bond

TO FULLY COMPREHEND THE ENDURING EXIS-
tence of the human and pet bond, we must consider the history of humankind. Prehistoric cave drawings and symbols
depict human beings hunting, feasting, and resting side by
side with animal companions. Intricate Egyptian statues and
art display humanity's fascination and love of the animal
kingdom. From the pet dogs and cats of early rulers to the
shepherd's herding dogs, people have found working and
loving relationships with the creatures surrounding their
existence. Animals have shared the company of our earliest
ancestors and undoubtedly will share many moons with our
future generations.

The interaction of human and animal began not as a
mere accident or need to complete daily work; it was a natural process of mutual interest from both human and beast.
Perhaps it began with a hungry beast's introduction to early

humans around a prehistoric fire. When the humans shared a meal with the animal, the animal protected the humans in return. The benefit of the mutual bond then developed into devotion and love. To these early humans, the beasts sharing the celestial earth seemed to serve a much greater purpose than assisting at the daily activities of hunt and survival. The animal extended unconditional love, enriched the lives of family members, and displayed playful friendliness.

The dependence we have on our pets has drastically changed since early eras of humanity. Today animals are rarely used for work in human survival, such as hunting for food or herding the family's flock of sheep. Now their roles are psychological; they are emotional stabilizers and family support. Our pets reflect the self-image and ego strength of us as individuals.

Relationships with Pets

Humans have a basic desire—and a need—to provide love and nurturing not only to each other and their offspring but to the surrounding world as well. During chaotic times of civilization, this fact may appear a fallacy, but each of us in some way has the need and acts accordingly. We see this desire demonstrated in the activities of children, who provide nurturing care to their favorite dolls, various toys, friends, and family. Adults exhibit similar traits, but with their children, friends, spouses, and pets. Pets fulfill a crucial purpose in our human lives.

It is impossible to express the joyous union born of having and caring for a companion animal. Objective comments do not offer a true definition of the infinite love people can feel for and give to pets. Pets offer us unconditional love and company, and the innocent, pure dependence we haven't experienced except in the earliest of childhood. When activities or incidents in our daily existence frustrate or worry us, our pet nudges us to give comfort and understanding. Pets can sense our distress, anger, and a variety of other emotions. They want to uplift our negative feelings.

No matter what type of individual we are—heterosexual or homosexual, black or white, assertive or timid, male or female—a pet thoroughly accepts us and never judges. This interaction intensifies for both human and animal. Each never fails the other, and a coupling develops unlike any other in the entire universe—an exchange of intimate enrichment evolves. It is as if the Gods placed animals upon this globe to live in harmony and love with humanity and share a divine relationship.

In our bond with our pets, we share the trials of life with another nonhuman creature, and in interaction with our pets we are our true selves. There is no need to display the false corporate flair necessary for a career at the office or the "expert Tarot card reader supreme" persona to those who doubt our ability. The tainted emotional responses we display from a hectic life within a chaotic society fade into nothingness as we share serene, loving time alone with our favorite pet. A pet's obedience makes us feel successful as individuals; their respect gives us the self-esteem and self-worth we rarely experience in objective life.

Our appreciation for their efforts, respect, and love unfolds in the way we assign them among the most personal valuables in our life. Some call their pet "my child" or "my best friend." Adults often refer to each other as their pet's "mom" or "dad," and children refer to their pet as a sibling or best buddy. As an expression of affection, some equate their pets to a relative or dearest friend and do whatever it takes to return the gesture of love. Many people spend grocery money on extra dog toys when FiFi already has the pleasure of twenty play toys, or they trade in a trip to the hair salon to have Sheba flea-dipped to relieve her suffering.

Touching Our Pets

We caress and pet our devoted companions with utmost freedom, and they reassure us by physically showing that they find great pleasure in our attention. In our human relationships, touching is usually discouraged or seen as wrong. Couples often shy away from displaying their affection in front of other people. Our ability to touch, caress, and physically display affection, however, is unrestrained with our pets. Ironically, humans accept this most readily. How many times have you seen people driving their car with the family dog in the front seat and a spouse or children in the back? A frequent sight is the affectionate kiss owners place on the head of their pet—whether in private or in public. This behavior and action is enormously enriching for us emotionally. It has been both medically and psychologically proven that blood pressure is reduced, heartbeat is improved, resistance to disease is heightened, and tension is eased (among other tangible benefits) just from caressing our pets.[1]

DEPENDENCE ON A PET

We enjoy our pet's adoration for who we really are. We unfold ourselves in complete openness to them, and we realize our interaction with our pets far transcends the relationships we have with other people. The familiar term "man's best friend," regarding a human's personal attachment to a dog, indicates the tremendous loyalty, trust, honesty, and development of security that is often beyond a level we can obtain from human friends, family, and even lovers or spouses.

Psychologists feel that in some cases people who depend on their pet so intensely and extend their private self exclusively to their pet are acting inappropriately; some pet lovers have forsaken some or much of their interhuman relationships for this sense of love and security.[2] When the world itself and other people are too threatening, condemning, or painful, these pet owners isolate themselves in an inner world consisting of themselves and their pet. Social interaction with other people can become handicapped by extreme dependence upon a pet for support. In the case of a troubled marriage or conflict between family members, one person may focus on the pet for the comfort of a trouble-free relationship and as a way of receiving support and love.

Although we may adore and love our pets, it is important to resolve conflicts and socially function with other people; we shouldn't rely so heavily on our special companions. To do so is unhealthy from a psychological standpoint, especially if the individual becomes a recluse. Such a dependence weighs so heavily that when a pet becomes lost or suddenly dies, the shock and void can lead to physical illness and serious mental health issues, including an inability to function properly in daily activities and social situations. If the death is gradual and expected, the dependent individual dwells exclusively on the pet's health and upcoming departure, leading to despair and depression that can last beyond the pet's death, sometimes perpetuating without resolution.

The selfish tendencies of many people can scar us in such a way that we seek out the intimate bond with animals and nature as opposed to other people, but to lead a fulfilling and productive life, we must love and care for ourselves and other people as well as our pets. At times I have found this difficult because of the wonderful relationship I have developed with Sasha, one of my dogs. Sasha has been with me for nine years, through hardships, emotional pain, joy, and triumph. The relationship reaches beyond any I've had with any person.

Many pagans found their religion as a result of condemnation from previous religious teachings, family members, and other forms of human interaction. The emotional upset and hurt of not being accepted by the people surrounding us may cause us to adhere to the sanctuary that nature unconditionally provides us, and the trusting love we receive from animals. Since our pagan beliefs are not widely accepted or welcome yet in the mainstream society, many of us are solitary practitioners who must rely on an intimate bond with nature and animals/pets to gain the support and spiritual encouragement that we otherwise should have from other people.

In order to survive in life we must deal with other people; we cannot lose sight of belonging to a larger social structure. Grasping hold of the human-pet bond as an escape or emotional buffer of the interaction we should experience with people leads to a vulnerable loneliness once the pet dies. Having been reclusive from other people, suffering the loss of a pet is made greater and more difficult to deal with than if we had the support of understanding people.

Many who practice pagan religious beliefs alone do so because they have interests and lifestyles that others consider eccentric or wrong. Besides a small circle of pagan friends (who may be separated by great distances), many pagans have no one to rely on. Though the Gods and Goddesses can lend spiritual comfort at such a distressful time as pet loss, we cannot ignore the importance of support and assistance toward resolution that other people can give.

Almost without exception, grief responses are most extreme when the bereaved has few or no significantly close human companions.[3] In a reaction to the absence of human understanding, the love of a pet evolves to an intensity beyond normal at the time of mourning. This is done to compensate for the absence of close relationships with other people. Usually the bereaved truly feels that retreating and drowning themselves in the lost relationship is justified and helpful. Such action can be unhealthy and makes the grieving process more difficult once reality catches up.

During my work as a Pet Grief Counselor, I prepared a funeral arrangement for a Doberman pinscher, an older woman's pet. The woman's children were grown and had moved away, and her husband seemed to exhaust her precious energies and emotions with his selfish needs. When her dog died suddenly of natural causes, the woman's only security in life was gone. Without the love and support of her husband and sympathetic friends, this woman went into a state of shock, emotional turmoil, and intense pain. Her health immediately became poor. In working with her to plan burial arrangements for her beloved dog, I saw that she needed professional help beyond my training. I recommended a few therapists and support groups, which she refused. She did not like most people and wanted to mourn alone.

In the days before the burial, she would call me, sobbing and obviously on the verge of a mental breakdown. I spent as much time with her as she needed—some of our phone conversations lasted two hours—to be certain she received support. I wanted her to know that someone was there for her and understood her pain.

On the day of the funeral, I met the woman and her husband in the wake parlor where the Doberman pincher awaited her inside a closed casket. I held the woman and we talked. Her husband stood carelessly across the room and glanced at his watch impatiently. I gently counseled the woman before lifting the casket lid. Once the casket was opened, I politely exited the room. I had been waiting inside my office for only a few moments when the husband threw open the office door and begged my assistance. The woman, whose sole dependence was on her faithful and loving pet, had gone into hysterics—she was convinced her dog was alive. She claimed her dog had looked at her (his eyes were closed) and his leg had moved. The woman was ready to lift the dog from the casket and exit the building. Her suffering wails prompted my supervisor to enter the room; it took us much time to comfort her and assure her of the pet's death.

Never before had I seen someone in such immense sorrow and trauma. The woman was an example of someone dependent on their pet beyond normal boundaries. No human companion in her life cared that she grieved; no family member or friend offered support before or after the death of her pet. Tears fill my eyes in remembrance. I kept in touch with the woman after her dog's burial and she eventually sought professional therapy, which gradually brought her through the devastating loss. She learned to cope in many aspects of her life.

In my experiences, I have found that every mourning individual who had total dependence on their pet contemplated suicide. Their religious practice, beliefs, or personality did not matter; they each verbally told me they considered suicide. I cannot stress to you the importance of taking such threats seriously. People whose lives revolve around their pet see their own life as completed—no longer livable and forever in despair—at their pet's death. If a grieving friend or relative tells you they are considering suicide, believe them and help them to obtain therapy. In many cases, in the individual's reality their pet may be a surrogate child, a mate for life, or a replacement human companion. In their reality, their pet was the only emotional support in life. Such individuals are the most self-destructive and should be properly treated by a professional therapist.

Pet Bereavement Awareness

The bereavement of our pets and its resulting psychological problems has launched a new social phenomenon in Western culture. We often take better care of our animal friends in the hope of extending their life than we do of ourselves. With so many individuals devoted to their animal companions, pet death care has become more practiced, recognized, and profitable. The evolution of pet-related industries has prompted recognition and public awareness, and the medical profession has begun to study this once-ignored bond between human and animal.

Grieving pet owners frequently ask me, "Is it really all right for me to mourn my pet so much? My friends and family tell me my pet was just an animal and I'm foolish to put myself through such distress." Although insight is being gained into this behavior, many people feel that mourning a pet's death is a ridiculous self-produced, self-deceiving trauma. Unless your human companions in life are "animal-people," they may dismiss your sorrow and criticize you. Rest assured, however, that mourning your pet is normal and should be recognized and dealt with in a healthy manner. You are most vulnerable during your mourning and many ignorant individuals offer discrimination as a symptom of their psychological inadequacy.[4]

The responses of criticism and ignorance are waning as our society recognizes and accepts the emotions associated with pet loss and offers assistance through the mental health field. Nonetheless, accept that at least one person will discount your grief and determine you are acting inappropriately.

When my cat Lester was tragically hit by a car, my neighbor called me at work and in tearful sobs informed me. I was shocked, devastated, and could not function enough to even respond. After a moment of silence, I thanked her for letting me know and said I'd take care of it. When I hung up the phone, I began sobbing and was so hysterical that my boss thought my parent, husband, or at least a human loved one had died. When he found out that my cat had died, he became aggravated. When I couldn't proceed with my work and requested a half personal day, he refused. Instead of being able to go home and remove my cat's corpse from the road and make necessary arrangements for her body, I had to stay at work where I could not mentally or physically function. My sympathetic co-workers told me they would finish my projects.

I telephoned a local animal control office and spoke with a nasty man who refused to pick up Lester's body. I was infuriated. After all, it was his job to remove animal carcasses from the roads. Attempting to remain calm, I resorted to pleading and asked that he simply put her body in a bag and leave her on the front porch of my home. He finally agreed. I then called my husband at work and asked if at his lunch hour he could take Lester's body to a pet crematorium to place on hold until I made arrangements for her cremation. Thanking the Goddess, it was done.

Depending on your personality, you may have handled the situation differently. I know individuals who have walked out and quit employment during such an incident. It is most important, therefore, that you consider ahead of time what arrangements you will conduct if such a tragedy should occur. Preparing now will help you deal with the final arrangements and grieving. There is nothing wrong with pre-planning your pet's burial or cremation (some options are listed in Chapter 7) and considering how you might best deal with the loss.

Remember that not everyone feels as you do concerning the human-animal bond. Unfortunately, many people will never experience the gratification, love, and personal happiness of loving a pet. The mutual love between pet owner and pet is a wonderful way to experience happiness in ourselves and our animal companions.

The unique bond many experience with their pet is a treasured part of their life. When a pet dies, a part of them dies at the loss of such an enchanting presence. Symbolically, pets are a living entity of our inner selves, personal thoughts, and true feelings. Therefore, it is justified to think that a part of us dies with a pet, but that part of us can be reclaimed through emotional relationships we experience with other pets and people. The mourning may take time to work through and even the religious beliefs of reincarnation or uniting again with our beloved pets in Summerland, or heaven, is not enough to comfort the emotional pain.

The Human Role in Mutual Bonding

The human role we play in the human-pet bond becomes a way of life, born of responsibility. Similar to the care and nurturing needed to raise a healthy, balanced child, the decision to have a pet is full of responsibilities. Throughout their existence, pets depend on the care of human companions; they never become independent as children do.

We each know of someone who owns a pet and is not responsible. This type of person infuriates sensitive pet owners and causes deep, emotional pain. We wonder why the person bothered to have a pet and why they don't give their pet away to a better home; some volunteer for animal rescue groups to stop the insanity.

Many pet owners, however, are reliable and accept total obligation for a pet's happiness, physical comfort, and health. These people's efforts are filled with passion and one of the kindest human acts of love. Pet owners who are also pagan religious practitioners are among the most sensitive ranks. The sensitivity to environmental issues, animal rights, and protecting the earth—not to mention worship of nature—prompts many to give all they can to the well-being of living creatures. For many pagans this is far beyond a common pet owner trait—it is a spiritual way of life.

Despite all of an owner's caring, no great acts of love and sensitivity can protect pets from the dangers of their existence. Even individuals who assume a god-like role in serving the well-being of their pets cannot halt accidents, illnesses, and death. Although pagan practitioners study and work magic with protective spells and healing rituals that halt accidents and illnesses to some degree, they must not assume god-like roles that will result in utmost despair when a pet's death occurs. Most pet owners inevitably suffer the false guilt that they somehow failed in responsibilities. This feeling must be recognized and reasonably dealt with. Many circumstances surrounding a pet's death can truly be out of a person's control and often cannot be comprehended.

Our Human Role as a Care Provider

Your role as care provider to your pet strengthens the bond you form with him or her. While caring for your pet relieves you from daily pressures, provides you with the joy of their presence, and a mutual exchange of love and pleasure, it can have its disadvantages as well. Your role of care provider and owner, which your pet depends on, has a psychological twist to it because you become dependent on your pet. This dependence gives you a sense of security, importance, and self-worth because your pet believes in you, needs you, and loves you. A strong foundation is formed in the human-pet bonding process.

In discussing the human role, it is important to note that the roles some individuals assume may be harmful. Providing sensitive care is not harmful; some individuals, however, go too far by considering themselves true "parents" of a "child" pet. They may dress up the pet in clothing, buy infant toys for the pet, provide stroller rides, or put their pet through excruciating hygienic trials that are unnecessary. These individuals mean no harm and believe they behave in the best interests of their pet. Sadly, this is not the case. Although it is impossible to know for certain if the pet likes or dislikes this overly excessive physical attention, there is cause for concern if the owner loses his or her grip with reality and the relationship becomes pathological.

OUR ROLE CONTINUES IN PET DEATH

A pet's death is a natural cycle in life. Intellectually, we know the Wheel of Life turns for them, as it does for all existence. Emotionally, however, you can never be ready enough. Not knowing for certain what happens at death causes a feeling of anxiety and sorrow when either a person or animal dies. We do not understand death and therefore find it difficult to accept. This is another reason the comfort and support of a human loved one is essential to help you through the intense feelings of failure, guilt, and anger.

Your human role in the bond with your pet perpetuates even after the time of death. You need to accept that your life must continue without your pet on the physical plane and provide care to yourself in order to cope. The loss must be endured. Besides the time, effort, and expense to make final arrangements for your pet, you have a demand within to make your pet's memory live on in a positive manner. Memorializing a beloved pet is a healthy step in the grieving process. I have done this by keeping the cremains of my cat Lester in a decorative urn and placing it on a handmade memorial shelf in our living room. Memorializing a pet is much like religious rituals conducted to obtain spiritual enlightenment and divinity. To forever hold the love for your pet, you need to allow for self-respect during mourning.

Allow your pet's living memory to help improve your life, which may have been shattered by his or her loss. Remember the wonderful enriching experiences you and your pet shared during their lifetime. Direct your energies to reminiscing about the joy and fond memories of your mutual love, instead of dwelling on the loss.

Elders and Pets

Our elders are very much mistreated and neglected by our society. It is easy to realize why their love for a pet can be enormous and fulfilling. Our elders enjoy relationships with pets in a special fashion because, although their health may be unstable, their pets still depend on and love them. This dependency renews their deteriorating sense of importance. As the five senses dwindle, depression can set in and savoring life ceases. When a loving animal companion provides love and happiness, however, it doesn't matter if the elder is ill or ignored by family.

Many of our elders have seen friends and family members die and have become more philosophical than in their younger years; that attitude helps them cope with the loss of a pet.[5] This is not to say that elders feel less sorrow, but rather that it is more easily coped with and best aimed toward a positive, earlier resolution. Certainly, the death is a shock that feels like abandonment, especially if the elder has no close human companions and it seems as if not even the Gods care. These emotions can lead to depression and further ill health, and it is essential that family, doctors, or social workers help the person to cope.

✦

Endnotes

1. Wallace Sife. *The Loss of a Pet* (New York: Howell Book House, 1993), p. 8.

2. Ibid.

3. Ibid., p. 9.

4. Ibid., p. 11.

5. Ibid., p. 18.

Chapter Two

The Bereavement Process

What Is Death?

BEFORE WE CAN LEARN OF AND UNDERSTAND the emotional responses of pet bereavement, we need to discuss the greatest mystery of life: death.

In civilizations that began in ancient times and still exist today, people have a different outlook of death than people living in modern civilizations. The ancient people of the world are not fooled by false claims that human beings can control nature. To these ancient civilizations, death is not a mistake or accident; it is a natural part of life.

The beauty of pagan spirituality is that it allows people to discuss, study, and recognize death as a natural stage of life. Religions such as Wicca teach the dark side of the Goddess, The Crone, who is not dark as in evil, but is considered dark in her reign of death and the gift of rebirth.

Rituals for birth, marriage, death, and rebirth (such as Initiation) are revamped within pagan religious practices and bring a new way to look at both life and death. Pagan religions teach that death is not to be feared, but to be accepted as a natural cycle of nature and all existence.

Life consists of change and transition. From the moment of birth, life is a journey leading to death. When was the beginning of you, me, and every sentient creature? It was not the day of birth, because we existed in our mother's womb previous to that day. Does each sentient being begin existence at the moment of conception? In my opinion, the reality is that our physical bodies were formed at conception, but not our unique, true self.

Each pagan religion has a theory concerning death. In Wicca, the soul is ageless and non-physical; it contains the essence of the Gods and Goddesses—the Creator. The soul travels the "Spiral of Rebirth" of life, death, and rebirth; reincarnated until perfection is obtained. When the cycle is completed, the soul returns for renewal and revitalization to the divine source from which it originated. With this idea in mind, life is similar to our waking time; death to our sleeping time: Although we never cease to exist, we temporarily withdraw from the waking experience. This is the process of rebirth.

In this whole context of the continuity of life, the Law of Karma operates. It is believed that the race, sex, place of birth, and other factors of a lifetime are determined by the soul's actions in a past life and the lessons learned. Karma is a tool and a law of action; it is the phenomenon that guides the soul in development. If you commit negative actions in this lifetime, negative actions will be returned to you. If you act positively in this lifetime, positive action will be granted to you. Each rebirth, based on these triumphs and failures of former lifetimes, provides the opportunity to reach potential and develop self. If your physical body ceases to function, or if you have physical death before enlightenment, your soul returns to earth in another physical body and continues the process of learning, seeking, and striving for the ultimate goal of enlightenment. Death, therefore, needs to be viewed as an advisor, not an enemy. Operating as an advisor of change, death prompts transition from one state of being to another. Every little change in life can be an example of death; change of what was before and rebirth of what it has now become.

The physical body ceases existence at death, but the soul lives on. Many pagan religions believe the soul travels to a nonphysical reality sometimes called Summerland. Certain pagans believe this reality exists without forms and that only energy beings coexist with the most superior of energy: the Gods and Goddesses. Other pagans consider Summerland a land of endless summer. The landscape and presence of nature is identical to that here on earth. Animals, people, plants—all sentient life—coexist in Summerland. In this nonphysical reality, the soul reviews the past life in a mysterious fashion, perhaps with deity. Lessons achieved or failed are reviewed. When the time is right, the soul returns to earth and life commences once more.

Initiation rituals of paganism symbolize a rebirth and spiritual awakening. These practices reflect what is thought to occur at physical death. In several pagan religious traditions, belief of what death consists of is derived from one or more of the three types of rebirth theorized by Carl Jung:

✦ *Metempsychosis,* or the transmigration of souls. The life force continues to exist and lives through different physical incarnations, which may be in human, animal, or plant form. Past lives cannot be remembered because the individual personality does not continue. Karma accumulated by each incarnation may affect future incarnations.

✦ *Reincarnation.* The continuity of the personality with life force that can be accessed by memory. The same ego-form existed in previous lives, present life, and can be recalled.

✦ *Resurrection* is the best-known belief of both ancient Egyptian and Christian religions. The ancient Egyptians believed that at the end of physical life the astral body functioned only if the physical body remained uncorrupted. The early Christians believed that the physical body lives again.

Aside from these three types of rebirth that follow physical death, Carl Jung theorized about two other kinds of rebirth that can take place during our lifetime and determine the afterlife of the soul:

✦ *Renovation,* or renewal, takes place at initiation. The initial initiation is a partial rebirth: the personality, or ego-form, is not changed but evolves in a new direction. Weak parts are strengthened, healed, and improved. The final initiation is a process of transmutation; it is a complete rebirth that changes the essence of a personality.

✦ *Indirect transformation* describes rebirth experienced through participation in mystery rites, such as seasonal rituals celebrating the transformation of nature and the inner transformation process of self.

Rebirth through these transitions determines the degree of a soul's perfection at physical death. Life force remanifests at death. Although the exact form of the manifestation is unknown, many theories exist. (Chapter 10 discusses the theories of death, particularly pet death, of several religions.)

Similar needs exist for all living creatures, including air, water, food, and a degree of warmth. Instinct, intelligence, and actions of living are obvious differences between humans and our animal friends, but nonetheless, we are all a part of the natural universe. The Wheel of Life affects us all. As all living creatures contain life force, are born, and physically die, it makes sense that animals have souls and make the transition to the afterlife. Perhaps for us the process of soul enlightenment and perfection is sought in incarnation, whereas our animal companions are not challenged with this goal.

Whether you believe in metempsychosis, reincarnation, resurrection, renovation, or transmutation in the spiritual world, there is no question your pet will make the journey to the afterlife and eternally remain in a loving bond with you through the spiritual realm.

The Bereavement Process

The focus of this chapter is the influence of culture on how we deal with pet death. You'll find a discussion on the many varieties of grief, including all the emotions experienced, from a psychological viewpoint. You'll learn how to meet each emotion courageously and aim toward resolution. Much of this information can also benefit you in the tragic loss of a human relative, friend, or companion. Many believe that the grieving processes for a pet and human life are similar. Some people are insulted by this comparison, but as we examine each phase of mourning you'll come to understand why the processes are similar.

The bereavement process begins with the initial discovery of death, and can last anywhere from a couple of days to several weeks or many months. Exactly how long you will grieve cannot and should not be measured or predicted. Each individual will react differently; there is no right or wrong time frame for mourning. People feel tremendous internal conflict and emotional pain during the grieving process. Often additional stress is caused by a need for approval to grieve so strongly for the loss of a pet. No matter the length of grieving, each person must be allowed the time and support needed to see them through the hardship.

As you move through the grieving process, you do not have to submit to overwhelming suffering. If you attempt to understand the psychological phases of grief, your responses to each one, and the mourning experience of other individuals, you can prepare yourself to face this process. Many people are fearful of the control death has over them and fear the grieving process itself. Not allowing their feelings to surface because of such fear can be emotionally harmful. The suppressed responses are real and devastating, and they must be released for healing to begin.

It is assumed that once a person deals with a first death—human or animal—that he or she will not mourn the death again and will resolve feelings quickly. This is not always the case. A current death often returns the emotional sorrow and stress felt at the first death. If the first death was not sufficiently dealt with, then it too will contribute to significant emotional upset. Usually that happens because it stirs up repressed and unresolved feelings that need to be dealt with and released.[1]

A woman who is a pagan of the Celtic religious practice called me one afternoon. Distraught, she said, "My cat Bobbi passed on to the Gods only two days ago and yet I no longer feel affected by it. Is this normal? Shouldn't I still be mourning? I loved him so much, yet the crying and sorrow has been lifted so soon. I feel guilty that I have quickly gotten over him."

Because of this woman's spiritual beliefs, pre-planned arrangements, cause of the pet's death, and other factors, her response was normal. The woman has enormous faith in her spirituality and believes in reincarnation; she knows she will reunite with her pet in the next life. Though she was hysterical for a little more than two days, her strong beliefs carried her through the grieving process. Also, Bobbi died of cancer, which the woman knew about. The death was not sudden and unexpected, which helped in her emotional preparation. During her religious and magical rituals, the woman calls Bobbi into her sacred circle, and she knows he comes. All these factors, and others, have made her grieving easier. Instead of an abrupt end, she considers her pet's death a transformation of their already existing relationship.

Separation Anxiety

When a pet dies, many owners suffer a degree of separation anxiety, which some psychologists regard as the key principle to the onset of the grieving process. The everyday normalcy of life is suddenly eliminated by the loss of a cherished pet. You feel alone, in a state of shock; your life seems empty and meaningless. As these initial feelings escalate, problems in both the psychological and physical world can also seem overwhelming.

Those individuals who grieve for more than a few days or seem to be unable to cope for months are also normal mourners. It is my opinion, however, that after a few weeks a great majority of the sorrow should be resolved. If depression is evident or the resolution has not occurred, the person must seek help in the form of support groups or a therapist because he or she does not seem to have the support and ability to cope themselves.

Psychological Reactions

Psychological reactions generally determine how long your mourning will prevail. The reactions need to be recognized and dealt with to begin healing.

The phases of the grieving process are shock and disbelief, denial, anger, solitude, guilt, depression, and resolution. These phases do not necessarily appear in a specific order and then disappear. All phases of grieving can appear in a different order than described in this text or may surface simultaneously. Because the grieving process is so personal and each individual reacts differently, it is impossible to clearly define the phases. We each have inner fears, religious beliefs, personality traits, and other internal factors that will not allow a precise definition.

One aspect to keep in mind, however, is that grieving is normal and is not a sign of neurosis, a mental disorder, or an act of extreme behavior. The response to grieve the loss of loved ones is natural and a completely healthy process so long as the mourner is not so distraught that they harm themselves or others. Guidance, understanding, support, caring, and someone compassionate with whom to speak about feelings are what is needed to sufficiently cope.

Symbolic values can distort grief significantly. Your deceased pet may have been cherished by a deceased friend, parent, or lover, or your pet may represent some special event in your life. Perhaps after an ugly divorce your pet was the only stable part of your life and you have depended on your pet's affection. In such cases, your pet is a living symbol of an aspect of your life extremely important to you. When your pet dies, the false sense of security is diminished and very often this can lead to an even more disastrous mourning process.

THE END OF AN ERA IN LIFE

The death of your pet marks the end of an era in your life. Once the phases of mourning are identified and resolved, there will still be aftershocks long after the mourning is concluded. It is normal to relive grief that was suffered years ago, or to have occasional sadness.

Several years ago, my rabbit died of a digestive problem of which I was unaware. I mourned him for nearly three weeks as I battered myself with guilt. A neighbor who had raised rabbits assured me that rabbits are fragile creatures and the health disorder from which my rabbit suffered was common and not easily detected. Her kind explanation and education enabled me to stop emotionally torturing myself. Although I resolved my tremendous grief, when I walked into a farm and feed store and came across a tub full of baby rabbits I painfully remembered my rabbit. But I smiled in tearful joy, recalling how my rabbit played with my dog Sasha, loved to burrow in my houseplant soil, and had an unusual fascination with my vacuum cleaner. To this day I can see him sweetly nudge me with his chin.

I can sympathize with the seemingly endless agony of heart, soul, and body at the loss of your pet. It does not seem fair that such wonderful, innocent, and loving creatures should have such short life spans. But then, we will have our special pets with us throughout our many years to chuckle in remembering their silly ways, or smiling at the thought of their greeting us when we come home. Death can be seen as a gracious relief for a cancer-ravaged pet or as a tragic, untimely unfairness at sudden death. The first, however, is not any easier to cope with than the last. Mourning is a lonely, emotional walk down the path of grief, but it will lead to the realm of resolution.

The Phases of Mourning

INITIAL SHOCK AND DISBELIEF

Often the discovery of your pet's death puts you into an initial degree of shock. Even individuals who knew their pet was dying of an illness or after a physically harmful accident experience shock and disbelief. You are completely at a loss of awareness and suddenly every aspect of your life is in turmoil. Inability to function physically or think clearly are sometimes the first signs an emotional overload is near. Powerful and overwhelming psychological reactions trip your thought processes and stun your mind. There may be a feeling of numbness in mind and body, or a sense of inability to physically react at all.

Some pet owners display unacceptance of the death and disbelief due to a powerful defense, which is a temporary phase. If you are faced with the death of a pet and you remark, "I can't believe it," at least you demonstrate that you have accepted the reality of the situation although it is overwhelming. Despite specific proof, some individuals repeatedly ask if their pet is truly dead, which is a sign that they have not accepted reality.

The mind's defenses are extreme and at times respond to the shock by acting oblivious to the circumstances. This mind-altering reaction is so powerful that you may seem hypnotized and unable to accept input that supports the overwhelming news. Some types of amnesia are caused by overwhelming shock and disbelief.[2] We hear reports of a person surviving a violent or extremely emotional trauma by blocking out the memories. Usually the memories surface suddenly and uncontrollably years later, but other individuals never recall what really happened.

No matter the defense maneuver, your mind is stalling because the circumstances are unbearable. The mind protects itself from having to deal with a sudden variety of tremendous, emotional issues. It is nature's last defense, shielding us from violence that can be done to the mind by unbearable stimuli.[3]

The temporary reaction of shock and disbelief, or unacceptance, will wear off only to be followed by other intense emotional reactions. Usually more than one emotion surfaces and can further the mind's distortions of the situation. Patience and time will lead to healing. These emotional responses are necessary to cope with the unexpected arrival of tragedy. You will feel helpless, violated, and dismayed for some time before you are able to appropriately cope with the separation anxiety.

When I recall the death of my beloved cat Lester, I can identify my brief period of shock and disbelief, which lasted almost four hours. I was soon capable of accepting her death, especially when my husband called me at work to say he had taken her body to the pet crematorium. I knew at that moment there was no possible error—my husband had seen her body and knew it was our pet. The shock waned.

Being able to accept your pet's death or loss, however, does not make the grieving easier.

As the grieving cycle turns, some behavior patterns develop that are not normal mourning reactions and can signal danger. Overreaction is common in many people; symptoms include fatigue, intensified irritability, sleeplessness, extreme withdrawal, excessive anger, antisocial behavior, and persistent nightmares and hallucinations of hearing or seeing the deceased pet.[4] (The nightmares and hallucinations do not apply, however, to the summoning of your pet in meditation, ritual, or welcome spiritual contact. It refers to the uninvited and hazardous symptoms of a mind nearing mental breakdown.)

When I was in elementary school, my family suffered the tragic loss of our elderly Labrador retriever, Sally. One night my mother let her outside to "do her business" and she lost her way in the darkness. My mother called and looked for her. Sally had wandered to a nearby road where she had been hit by a car. The driver was a neighbor, and I remember her coming to our house crying with the news. My mother was horrified and shocked. The woman was near hysteria, and we had to console her as well as deal with our initial shock. I was not allowed to go with my parents to the accident scene, but my parents went and took Sally to the veterinarian. When they arrived home, Sally was bandaged and severely injured. She suffered broken ribs and an array of serious injuries. The veterinarian had said if she did not eat, drink, or appear strong in a day or two he strongly recommended euthanasia (putting Sally to death by injection, in this case). Sally did not improve, and my family agonized at watching her suffer. She was put to sleep two days later.

Days and weeks after Sally's death, I experienced strange sensings of her. At night I heard Sally's claws clicking across the kitchen floor as if she were walking about the house. On two of these occasions I got out of bed in the middle of the night, and as a child, had a spark of hope that she had indeed risen from the dead or was somehow home alive. I thought I saw Sally on many occasions—rounding the corner from the kitchen into the living room, sitting in a corner, and walking outside in our yard. This was very frightening for me as a child.

This type of abnormal response indicates post-traumatic stress syndrome and should not be ignored if it occurs frequently enough to disrupt the sufferer's life. Although my hallucinations eventually stopped, many psychologists and medical professionals believe that the experience does not go away but is suppressed. Post-traumatic stress syndrome will remain until adequately dealt with through the intervention of a professional psychologist. Otherwise, the syndrome will fester and possibly create excessive problems in the person's life. I cannot stress enough that professional help is necessary if this type of problem occurs relentlessly. The release of repressed psychological disturbances must be done.

Not everyone suffers this phase of grief. Many people are already emotionally injured or dealing with enormous stress in their lives. The impact of another trauma may simply be too overbearing for the individual to cope with alone. Normal shock and disbelief are reasonable responses that are not unusual in their own right. These responses should disappear rather fast as new problems surface.

The intense emotional stress you suffer during your mourning can cause you to question your sanity. You should not worry about your sanity as long as you are coping. There will be temporary agony, but the responses all should wane through healthy coping. Only when post-traumatic stress syndrome, depression, thoughts of suicide, denial, or other destructive emotions surface and remain is professional help necessary.

DENIAL

Denial is another early phase of grieving and is often confused with the disbelief that accompanies the shock of learning about the death. Denial is different because it produces disillusionment and a loss of reality. Individuals suffering denial cannot cope sufficiently and alter reality to reject the notion of death altogether and save themselves from the normal, mandatory experience of mourning and resolution. Denial is total rejection of the reality of the situation and refusal to believe. Within the realm of denial, an individual may acknowledge the death has happened, but attempts to refute it.

Denial typically develops after the initial shock and disbelief and sometimes after other emotional responses, such as guilt or anger. The devastating finality of death causes some individuals to approach it as a bad dream or something that is unreal. The strong passion to believe the pet is still alive and all will be well again is a stumbling block in the grief process that recedes once the grim reality returns. For most people, denial is brief and is resolved quickly.

Initial denial plays a role in a protective exercise that allows the mind to rest in painless limbo for a short time. Denial is typically short-lived because other realities intervene and force the fact of death and the need to cope back to our attention. As you experience denial and then acceptance, you proceed through the developmental phases of the grieving-healing process.

The abnormality and greatest concern of denial occurs when an individual is convinced that something can be done to return the lost life. For example, an individual may strive to locate a missing pet, when in reality the pet is deceased. The individual believes that the pet's physical disappearance has been caused by something other than death.

Denial does not include the healing techniques of meditations, rituals, and afterlife belief. Religiously speaking, it is healthy to consider your pet spiritually alive and existing upon the spiritual plane; ascending toward divinity for reincarnation, transmutation, or resurrection; and believing communication with your pet is possible. You are celebrating your belief and accepting that your pet has crossed the threshold from physical existence into the realm of death. Performing rituals to aid in your healing or acts of communication between you and your deceased pet are healthy ways of coping.

Concern arises, however, when an owner denies the fact that a pet has crossed the threshold into the realm of the Gods and continues to believe the pet lives, even though they have personally witnessed the evidence of his or her death. When faced with death, some individuals become disillusioned into believing that the "disappearance" of the pet was caused by the attending veterinarian or another individual (perhaps someone who witnessed the death). Whenever an individual shows this type of behavior by an unwillingness to accept or acknowledge the physical death of a beloved pet or insisting someone has committed a conspiracy, professional intervention is essential. This behavior is beyond the normal unacceptance resulting from initial shock and disbelief.

During my career as a Pet Grief Counselor, I dealt with this rare but existing dilemma. One woman could not accept the physical death of her dog. She telephoned me frequently to discuss her anger and resentment toward her lawyer, veterinarian, and her family because they refused to help her uncover the conspiracy behind her dog's sudden disappearance. Knowing that her dog was indeed deceased and on hold in the pet cemetery's freezer, I attempted to gently coax her into the realization that her dog had died of natural causes as found in the autopsy and to tell her I was personally handling her dog.

The more I reassured the woman, the more angry and denying she became. I recommended professional intervention to her husband, who wept for his wife and told me she refused. The woman's life was dedicated to unveiling a conspiracy that did not exist. She was no longer mentally living in our reality. On the day of her dog's wake and burial, the woman began to accept the reality. Perhaps actually seeing and touching her beloved dog and witnessing his burial process provided the evidence her mind required. Considering the fact that this woman refused professional therapy, she and her family were fortunate that the act of holding a wake and attending the arranged burial was enough to bring her through her unhealthy denial.

Through studies conducted of human psychology and the mental health field, it has been discovered that people experience two types of denial: bargaining and fantasy.

Bargaining Denial: Often the immediate responsibilities, such as the care of the pet's body, have been performed when bargaining denial begins. Usually you are alone and smothered in grief, feeling frustration and a sense of helplessness.

You sense your pet's presence still in your home and you anticipate the familiar sight of your pet napping by a favorite chair or playing in its cage. There is a surrounding void in your home and a feeling the home environment is no longer real—as if a time warp or temporary loss of reality has been experienced. In your helplessness, frustration, and confusion, you consider that perhaps your pet isn't deceased and life may revert to the way it was. Once your hopes dwindle, the bargaining evolves. Perhaps you bargain with your deity so your pet will return. "I'll be a better person," or other messages are whispered to the Gods in the hope that goodness in your future behavior will be traded for the renewed life of your pet. This type of denial is a psychological function of need from your mind through the bargaining process. If your pet's death is expected, such as in the case of terminal illness, this denial might play an impassioned role before the actual death. It never works, and the fact of death still remains.

Fantasy Denial: In a childlike state of pretending, you may toss your pet's toys upon the floor with the notion that somehow your pet will come running to play and be with you again. You might fill water and food dishes. These fantasies are beautiful displays of love, but you need to remember that they are not real. Your pet has died and time moves you onward through life. Whether you put effort into resolution or not, you will go on.

Both bargaining and fantasy denial are typical if you did not witness your pet's death. You may have heard the news from a neighbor or family member or, in a gesture of love, the witnesses may have disposed of your pet's body. Although this gesture is kind and meant to be helpful, in the long run it may cause you to have difficulty in accepting the reality. "Where is my pet's body?" "Did you actually see what happened?" "Maybe it wasn't my pet—maybe it was someone else's that you thought was mine." A stranger may even have been the messenger, and it seems appalling that a third party to such a personal, loving relationship should inform you. The stranger is not welcomed, and you may feel it is somehow wrong that this person has told you something so intensely personal.

With the pet owner's emotional state in mind, many veterinarians have become educated and sensitive to the denial stage of grieving. Usually the education is through common sense and experience. Your veterinarian, if truly an animal lover and care provider, will be your closest ally in the battle of resolution. Normally your veterinarian views the body of your pet and has a role in arrangements that you desire to make for burial or cremation. The loving veterinarian will know that the first stage of grieving should be conducted in privacy, somewhere in the clinic or hospital, between you and your deceased pet.

Veterinarian teaching hospitals train their personnel to handle the pet owner's grief and initial emotional responses. One of the most important principles is that the pet owner should view their pet's body if possible and receive utmost assistance in making arrangements for the body as well as getting emotional support. Your veterinarian should extend this service, which can be assessed by your noting his or her bedside manner.

Though the veterinarian staff means well, often grieving pet owners avoid the offer of emotional support. As the technician attempts to console, the pet owner stands rigid and role-plays a calm, emotionally strong and collective persona. Anyone who has worked with people and animals through a pet death knows that the individual amplifies this type of behavior from fear—fear of their own responses, fear of the finalization of death, and fear of the self-confrontation that must follow.

Because human beings are often trained to avoid the ultimate reality of death, we give ourselves excuses to practice denial. We understand that death comes to all living things, and yet our human society teaches that talking about it and thinking of it are taboo.

Such a defense mechanism as denial is justifiable and valuable when it serves as temporary protection from overwhelming problems. Your human mind practices such defense mechanisms whenever a painful reality exists that offers too much too soon and psychologically we need a time out. Immediate and full acceptance at the time of a death is nearly impossible. Each individual will express denial differently. Tolerance and patience are crucial during the hardship of making the transition.

As a pagan spiritualist, you have spiritual tools to assist you throughout this transition and the entire process of grief. In most pagan spiritual beliefs, there is an understanding that death is a cycle of life and, like the changing seasons of nature, it is both inevitable and unable to be rationally denied. You realize that as each day passes, all life grows closer to the threshold of death. The spiritual plane awaits all living creatures, and there is no given time of when the threshold will be crossed. Sudden death of a loved one may cause a temporary sense that the untimely ascent to the spiritual world is not justified, but you know that the transition from physical existence to the spiritual world is one of growth, evolution, and promising rebirth. Rebirth may be in the form of transmutation, reincarnation, or living a spiritual existence among the Gods. You do not need to deny your pet's experience of the glorious, divine, and beautiful transition into the realm of your deity. Your pet has succeeded physical existence and further evolves in spiritual existence. Denying that physical death has occurred will only cause internal misery for you. Remember that your pet lives on in the spiritual world capable of communication with you. The transition of your pet's being is a cycle of his or her life. It is a new beginning in your pet's existence and an inevitable cycle to be experienced in your loving relationship.

In extreme cases of denial, you may feel pushed by other people or criticized harshly, and may begin to intensify other underlying concurrent psychological problems. The best help is to allow yourself to hold on to the denial until you are ready to let go on your own. The only exception is if there is a psychological risk, in which case you need professional counseling or at least involvement with a support group. If the problem of denial is excessive and unyielding after much time, let a professional evaluate the situation.

Anger

Being unable to understand death or have a sense of control in a pet loss situation may cause you to experience intense anger and outrage. You may distribute anger and frustration at random and create excuses to vent rage at other people. This anger can be projected outward or dealt with internally. Sometimes, when guilt or self-blame prevails, you may even assign responsibility and inflict blame onto others.

The total helplessness you feel at the death of your loved one is frustrating, yet you must deal with your anger in a healthy fashion. More often than not, people incorrectly deal with anger. Your pet's life is snatched from your loving embrace and the special relationship, unlike any other you may experience in life, is suddenly gone. Immersed in the sorrowful passions of bereavement, anger is much more difficult to handle and resolve than in many human conflicts or circumstances.

For a time, you may feel anger toward your God or Goddess. While you may accept such theories as reincarnation, transmutation, or resurrection, you may be wondering why your pet had to die now. Although you may understand that your pet is unified with you through spirit, it is normal to feel angered at the loss of caring for your pet in physical existence. Your role of care provider, friend, and beloved part of your pet's physical life has not ended but has transformed into a new type of loving relationship upon the spiritual plane. The doctrines of pagan religious belief systems offer answers and considerations for the crossing from physical death to the spirit world, but for a time these doctrines may not seem enough to quench the anger of the loss.

Your anger is probably not based on a lack of devotion to the theory of death you hold; in your spiritual practice, you know that death is a continuation of life, not a disposal of it. Death reminds us that all living creatures upon earth, the physical plane, are fragile and meant to exist only for a time. Regardless of the religion you follow, emotions at your pet's loss will surface—and these emotions will differ from person to person.

Many times, the devotion and reverence to nature and the recognition that all creatures are sentient life assist the pagan practitioner in coping with the grieving process. We understand the cycles of nature and the Wheel of Life of birth, death, and rebirth. We realize and accept that the Crone's symbolism in the Wiccan religion's Triple Goddess aspect allows death to be an important part of pagan religious practice and therefore can benefit us superbly when we need to overcome anger.

Some individuals equate a pet's death with being taken. Loss of perspective of right and wrong seems unavoidable at this time. A person's sense of proportion can be distorted from the frustration and rage of such an untimely or violent sense of loss. Be aware that regardless of your religious ideology, this distortion is sometimes impossible to avoid. At this stage of the mourning process, situations that normally would be trivial or meaningless are suddenly exaggerated and misconstrued in our passionate need to assign blame to someone or something.

Keep in mind that although anger is termed "irrational" in a psychological analysis of loss due to death, we are human beings. We are emotional creatures living longer lives than many of our beloved animal neighbors. A certain amount of anger is to be expected; you should not feel guilty or unworthy in feeling anger toward death. When we as human beings cannot fully and rationally understand something, we can become confused, bewildered, and angry.

Any God, Goddess, or person within our lives can be made into a scapegoat for our anger at this trying time. Often the veterinarian and hospital staff involved in a pet's health care and death arrangements are the first to be blamed as we express anger. Deep within, you know these people are acting appropriately in attempting to help your animal companion and have your pet's best interests at heart, but your helplessness and search for answers to death may cause you to blame them wrongfully.

During this stage of mourning, it is also common for you to internalize anger. You may blame yourself for a variety of weaknesses, faults, and decisions at the inability to prevent your pet's death or to sustain a dying life. If you are forewarned and prepared for such a response, you can lessen the negative effects. Anger must be recognized and resolved for what it truly is under these circumstances: an irrational exercise in self-defeatism.

When we find moments or subjects in life that are confusing or make us feel helpless, meditation and ritual can unfold our minds to new realization. Anger may be a conscious, first response to something we don't understand or can't control. In meditation we can bring anger forward, examine the emotion from many angles, and diffuse it through understanding and knowledge within the higher self. Reaching toward the higher self is a great act of self-help. Attempts of self-defeatism are then replaced by regaining control and obtaining perspective. Healing—coupled with guidance sought from the God or Goddess—can uplift us from the struggles that anger creates when balance, understanding, and overcoming negative emotion is so crucial.

Feeling overwhelmed by your emotions at this time is common. You are vulnerable as you lose perspective in your involvement. At other times in life, you would not be as upset by circumstances and events that now cause you to display anger or rage. Self-destructiveness is the only outcome of the potent force of withheld anger.

Become able to let go of this anger. Your higher self, guidance of your deity, and faith are tools that can assist you. This subjective response is an intensely personal one that requires you to be honest with yourself. Keeping anger submerged is not the answer. You deserve much better in mourning.

The anger assessment exercise helps you to let your anger surface into an objective state and release it. You are the best source to help yourself through this difficult moment in time, but helping yourself requires the utmost truth from within.

Anger Assessment Exercise

Conduct this exercise within your religious or magical sacred space or during a quiet moment of privacy. Do this exercise over the course of a few days. Attempting to finish it in one sitting will result in further frustration and impatience.

What You'll Need: a pencil or pen, a sheet of paper, and the intention of being totally honest with yourself.

Difficult as it may be, try to clear your mind of the overwhelming emotions of your loss. Meditation will help you clear your thoughts and focus. Your goal is to recognize the anger that you are experiencing and strive toward resolution. Take as much time as needed to maintain as calm a state of being as possible.

Once ready, write the word "anger" at the top of the sheet of paper. Now make a list of the people and places that are causing your anger at this time, using the following statements as a guide:

✦ List the people toward whom you feel anger.

✦ List the people who have upset you in some way throughout your bereavement.

✦ After each name, write a brief sentence describing why you are angry at that person and the ways each person has caused you additional distress.

✦ List the places (such as the veterinary hospital or workplace), situations, and any other individual or occurrence you feel has caused you additional stress during this time.

After careful consideration and completion, put this list aside and allow a few days to pass before examining it again. This lapse of time will allow you greater objectivity.

When you read this list again, concentrate, one by one, on each named source that has caused you additional discomfort and pain. People in your life who are insensitive and make hurtful comments regarding your mourning have caused you real pain. Consider if there is a reason in their own lives that prevents their understanding of the loss you face. Could a person causing you discomfort have a problem facing death, which is the cause of their callous attitude toward you? Because of your grief and anger, could you be making these individuals into additional problems for yourself? Is one person the target of your upset? Are you ready to forgive those individuals who simply are not animal people and have no idea what it is like to have a loving relationship with animals? Can you forgive those people who simply cannot relate, or understand, or who say inappropriate things to you?

In the case of your anger toward your veterinarian or hospital staff, could it be that they tried to sustain your pet's life to the best of their ability and cannot be held accountable for what was destined to be? Could your anger at your animal care providers be due to your emotional turmoil at needing someone or something to blame?

When we hurt the most, we inflict our rage and pain upon those people who truly matter in our lives and somehow, it is felt, failed in helping us when we needed their support. Often when we sit crying and hurting, we so desire the love and understanding from all who are within our lives, and some people simply cannot provide for our expectations or desires.

Consider the valid excuses people might have to offer for their responses to your grief. For example, if a pet died of a terminal illness, a loved one might say, "Fluffy is better off dead. You should be grateful and cry tears of joy!" But in mourning the comment could be misinterpreted as, "Who cares that Fluffy is dead. Don't cry about it." Recognize the difference between what was actually meant by the comments and what you heard as a result of your mourning. During this time, it will ease your pain if you can learn more about yourself and your anger through this type of objectivity.

Some individuals simply have their own fears of death and it is uncomfortable for them to comment. Another person may not be able to comment at all because they don't know what to say to make you feel better. It is not that they do not understand, sympathize, or care in most cases; they are probably afraid that discussing death will upset you further.

Realistically, there may be absolutely no reason for you to be angry at others. Perhaps you are really angry at yourself, or there may be a real reason for the anger you are unwilling to recognize and deal with appropriately. You need to be honest and frank with yourself during this self-examination.

When anger evolves within us, it is difficult to think clearly and easy to erroneously identify problems or overreact. If a loved one or friend states that you are overreacting in anger, it may hurt your feelings, but it may be true. It is important to discover what else is subconsciously upsetting you to cause your overreaction, and resolve that as well.

Anger is a reaction—usually an instant action—to a perceived violation or offense, and is extremely personalized. Anger does have legitimate uses, but can be abusive. We must wonder if we can or need to be angry at death and our reality. You need not be angry with yourself for being unable to defeat death or to fully understand it. Memorializing your pet cannot be done in a positive manner with anger. Luckily, this phase of mourning will disappear if you allow yourself the time to cope, have patience from others, and permit it to pass.

SOLITUDE

Solitude is a safe haven we create to get away from others or deal with the ridicule from ignorant individuals. When grieving, solitude is not the same as withdrawal, which we will discuss later. You may seek solitude because you do not know how to react to those around you during this confusing, sorrowful, and resentful time. You may tell yourself that your co-workers, family, friends, and even your spirituality cannot help or comfort you. You may find yourself drowning in suffering, misinterpreting the responses of others, producing unexplained barriers, and refusing any help.

As you deal in daily activities and decision-making with people during grieving, you often react with rash actions that you may regret later. Those people who seem judgmental about your grief catch you off balance and you can lose perspective.

When a pet dies, you may find yourself seeking privacy and silence because you are fearful of ridicule and criticism from others. Statements people make that seem insensitive include, "It was just a pet—so get another. It'll make you feel better" or "Why are you so upset about a pet? It's just an animal, not a person." You may be told that by mourning your pet you are overreacting, which is not true. When your emotional strength has plummeted, and your feelings of guilt and sorrow arise, you are often unprepared to handle such commentary constructively.

You may wonder how people can make such cruel comments when they do not fully understand the circumstances that led to your pet's death, or the special, intense relationship you had with your pet. Does it make these people wrong to attempt to state a legitimate point from their limited perspective? If a person cannot accept your mourning for your pet, they will continue to disappoint your needs and expectations at this trying time.

The criticism from others causes your defense mechanism of anger, which in turn may cause you to seek solitude. If you cannot speak your mind and disagree with their comments, you will surely justify alienation for a short time because you do not want to see, hear, or have any contact with that person.

At this vulnerable time, you are seeking an outlet for your powerful, brewing emotions. You are psychologically imbalanced by grief and trying to cope. You need to keep in mind that even the relationships strained by someone who cannot help you at this needy time have positive value and significance. If you allow yourself to be hurt by their lack of understanding or compassion, you defeat yourself. If you punish them with angry words or permanent alienation, you may regret it later.

Some human beings consider animals as pets, mere childish playthings, a waste of time and expense, or possessions like any other piece of property. They have every right to hold these opinions just as you have every right to disagree. These people's agitated and insensitive behavior regarding your energies spent on mourning your pet's death may reflect their fear to contemplate death.

To your amazement, some individuals closest to you may offer no response at all during your bereavement. Their silence is demeaning. You may mistake their absence of a caring, supportive statement as a critical commentary. In your anger and grief, you don't stop to think that the silence may exist because your close human companion does not know how best to respond.

We forget in mourning that death is a frightening and threatening subject for many people. People in your life may not be able to discuss it without feeling these emotions. Despite your breaking heart and need for their support, you cannot push or demand consoling. If you love and respect these people, you must realize they are human too and are incapable of helping you cope because of their own fright and uncertainty.

How can you positively respond to other people in such situations? If a perceived assault upon your grief happens, you usually make one of the following three responses:

✦ You snap angrily with bitterness.

✦ You are put off guard in such a manner that you don't know what to say. You say nothing in your embarrassment or confusion, which gives the impression you are not disagreeing with or contradicting their statement. Many times this second response comes from interaction with a supervisor or boss at your workplace or someone in authority who has stated something you are not ready for and has caught you at a disadvantage.

✦ You respond with your preplanned statement.

When an insensitive person strikes, have a planned response ready such as, "In my opinion, you are not an animal person and have probably never experienced the special bond you can have with a pet. You do not understand the love, understanding, and companionship my pet gave to my life. Please do not be so judgmental and intolerant as I feel the deep, personal feelings of loss at this time."

Say something to that effect with a calm but firm voice. You do not want to seem offensive or defensive. Keep in mind that this person has no clue what it is like to feel as you do, or they wouldn't have been so insensitive. In a work environment, remain calm and tolerant within yourself when dealing with such people. Bursting into an angry, defensive rage will only cause your superiors to question your ability to handle your job through this personal crisis and future ones.

You want to exhibit nonthreatening responses that make your feelings clear. By maintaining your respect and enlightening people who may not understand the intensity of your grief, you could save a valuable relationship. In fact, it could save you from suffering further emotional upset. Irrational reactions do not straighten out rude or insensitive individuals, but cause delay in your healing and your ability to cope in your life without your pet. Concentrate on those people who are sensitive to your loss.

Solitude to reflect on your relationship with your pet and tearfully mourn is healthy, but solitude in avoiding people who may criticize you is not healthy.

GUILT

Within intense bereavement, you may feel guilt that you somehow failed in your obligation to your pet. In your care for animals, you take on a moral presumption—your pets are totally relying on you. You are honored to have the duty and provide care for all aspects of your animal's life. When the unexpected and unwanted tragedy of death or other loss of your pet ends your duties, you may accuse yourself of personal inadequacy. Your emotional responses somehow send messages that you have failed to perform as well as you could have. In some cases, a person feels that this inadequacy caused their pet to die.

Guilt is an emotion related to shame and both are born of a negative response that could have been averted. Guilt is based on insecurity or a negative self-evaluation and is a normal response to failing some duty or obligation.[5] Guilt, however, is not the same as disappointment. Guilt admits to failing at a level well within our competence. Scientific research and professional analysis concludes that guilt is a human emotion that is not observed in wildlife. However, in training and scolding our pets for violating an expected or proper behavior, we've extended this emotion to them. When scolded, a dog will lie down some feet away, staring back at us with saddened eyes, and eventually approach and nudge us in apology.

When investigating the causes of guilt, examine a key principal to owning and caring for a pet: responsibility. You are completely responsible for your pet's nutrition, medical attention, quality of life, sexual status, playmates, whereabouts, and more. Your pet becomes dependent on you and you become emotionally dependent upon him or her. The bond is one of the purest give-and-take relationship forms. Your human responsibilities cease to exist at your pet's death and you may become victim to your own mind—the creation of a sense of guilt derived from the loss of responsibility and irrational thoughts that you did not carry out previous responsibilities appropriately. Often, you failed to be in control of the situation involving your pet's death or other loss. You were unable to protect him or her and, in your reflection, you believe you must have been able to do something. "If I had taken Penny out for her morning walk at the usual time, she would not have seen the cat, chased it into the road and been killed! How could I let this happen?" Because of your pet's dependence, you tend to lead a god-like role in their lives. Remember to recognize that you are fallible and though your efforts extend love, you are not capable of controlling fate and the random hazards of existence.

In many cases, the feeling of guilt arrives in the earliest stages of mourning, after disbelief and before anger. These emotions are so powerful that they can distort all attempts at objective thinking. Your mind pours forth the dwelling of fantasy: "I should have…" "I could have…" and "If only I had…." You begin to believe that your actions or inactions were insufficient. As humans we strive for what we cannot reach and desire outcomes beyond our abilities and skill.

When my cat Louis died after being hit by a car, I mentally battered myself with accusations of irresponsibility. I asked myself how I could allow him to be an indoor/outdoor cat when I knew the risks. How could I be so negligent as to allow his outdoor activity when a highway was close by? The truth of the matter was that Louis once was an indoor cat, but after the day he slipped outside and got a taste of nature, he threw cat tantrums (including knocking things off of tables and literally climbing the walls) until I let him out again. He wanted to live exposed to nature and it was better for him to live five years of cat adventures and enjoyment of nature than a lifetime shut in the house against his desires.

On the night of Louis' death, however, I could not consider these truths. I kneeled on the earth before his home burial site, sobbing. My anger and guilt led to terrible upset; I demanded that the Gods give me a reassuring answer, once and for all, about what death is. Would I ever see Louis again? Is he now transformed and existing in another realm unknown to me? Is he just gone—his existence swallowed up in time like a black hole? Even my spiritual beliefs of death did not matter in my early grief.

I resolved my anger, guilt, and emotional pain by writing poems of my love for him. I wrote what he meant to my life, and my emotional trauma over his death. Through writing these poems I released many internal emotions, uncovered hidden personal problems adding to my distress, revealed irrational reaction, and started my way toward resolution.

In the whirlwind of emotional upset through bereavement, it is expected that you will blame yourself or others. Through this, there is a sense of regained control. But applying blame makes little sense because it never existed. To many, however, it makes a difference emotionally. We feel better assigning blame to the physical plane where we have control, and not acknowledging that death is a fact of life we must learn to accept.

Thinking of what you could have done only punishes you while you are already in anguish. We wonder why life is sometimes so cruel and we dwell, without purpose, on how we could have postponed, prevented, or eased our pet's death. Digression into this thinking only results in significant pain and no resolution. However, healthy analysis of what happened can add to personal growth and result in a better future lifestyle.

Guilt is unfounded, no matter the circumstances. You are your worst critic because you search desperately for an explanation of why death or loss came now.

Pagan philosophy recognizes the concept of no guilt—no blame, but our rationality becomes somewhat lost during mourning. Although we understand the Wheel of Life and the concept that death is a part of life leading to a rebirth, in grief these beliefs do not seem enough. Some individuals want a material answer and assigning guilt to self or blame to others seems the only way to get an answer.

During bereavement, many people, regardless of their spiritual beliefs, seek out immediate answers of death, questioning their beliefs and the meaning of life. No matter how we examine death, it will not make sense that an innocent, trusting, loving animal must die. You may consider all the hate crimes, criminals, and bad incidents in humanity and wonder why the Gods or the Universe would destroy or rid the earth of such a loving, accepting, and pure creature. In this, we must realize that because we do not have definite answers of what death is, we automatically attribute negative traits to it. Death could be the most beautiful part of a creature's existence. You must have faith that death is what all the ancient scriptures and religious texts from around the world philosophically define it as—a divine, wonderful transition where physical pain and suffering are no more.

In certain individuals, the perpetual feeling of guilt is a way of life, and they think that self-punishment is well deserved for what or who they are. They derive an emotional payoff from their guilt, albeit a negative one, because they are already vulnerable and suffering in some way internally. There is no positive service in this, and they only hurt themselves more with this guilt. If you are this type of person, stop punishing yourself. You are a caring, loving individual who has suffered the loss of your pet—give yourself compassion, not punishment. Console yourself as you would a human loved one who suffers the same. Take this time to give yourself tender loving care and continue loving your pet, who I assure you has nothing but continuing love for you—not blame.

Circumstances such as a cat escaping through an open door or window, a dog running into the road, or a pet eating a poisonous plant are not uncommon. Feelings of guilt may seem justified by thinking the death of your pet was untimely, or that something could have been done. But consider this: it may have been time for his or her death. Accidents happen and you do not need to blame yourself by assuming you could have done something to prevent it.

When loss happens and there was no time to say goodbye, you may feel cheated and particularly upset. What you desired was to see your pet's natural death and give a loving farewell. Realize that you have limited control over fate. Philosophers and wise men and women have claimed all that happens is natural, whether or not by accident.

When accidental death happens, we feel there is plenty of evidence we failed. There are horrifying accounts of pet owners accidentally causing the death of their own pet. One woman threw out the garbage and later found her kitten dead; her pet had hidden inside the garbage bag in play. Antifreeze dripping from vehicles claims many pet lives, and pet owners punish themselves with guilt. Death can occur during the application of anesthetic at the veterinarian clinic; this is usually caused by an underlying health problem, such as a heart rhythm disorder, that went unnoticed. All of these examples seem preventable, but as people we must accept that we cannot control all life flawlessly. In our care for ourselves and our pets, we try to improve the odds for survival, which is all we can realistically do.

Wishing things were different through guilt wastes your energies and livelihood, and perpetuates negative energy within yourself. We are human beings and we make mistakes. If not done on purpose, don't we deserve compassion, forgiveness, and a letting go of the pain? There is no room for questioning yourself about what preventive measures you could have taken because you need to accept the reality of your pet's death and continue living and loving. Allow yourself to let go—show yourself compassion. It is a difficult effort, and this takes time and patience.

A wise Wiccan practitioner said to me at a Samhain ritual, "Religion exists to help humanity cope and feel better about death." If you think about the purpose of religion, you can see some truth to her words, but we question our religion and ourselves when we search for direct answers. To add to the questioning, many religious denominations do not offer explanation, support, or discussion of an animal's role in human existence, much less where their souls travel at death.

When I was a child, my family attended Sunday morning sermons at an Episcopal church. One morning the minister discussed animals as God's creatures. He stated that animals, unfortunately, do not have souls. My father was clearly uncomfortable with that statement. After the sermon, he approached the minister and asked him if he thought animals went to heaven or had an afterlife. The minister answered "no." My father said that he did not need to go to heaven if there would be no animals. Our family never went back to that church.

Not all religions or people believe animals have souls or an afterlife. But if you doubt either, think about this: Animals breathe air to live as we do. Their physical bodies and minds are similar to our own. They require air, water, food, and survival instinct to live. In my thinking, humans are arrogant to believe only we have souls or are the only creatures of worth on this planet. As all living creatures have life-force, we all experience afterlife.

Do not feel guilty that you believe you and your pet will share afterlife together if your religion states differently. It is not wrong for you to love your pet, even more than most people, or desire to reunite in afterlife. Science and religion understand so little about life, much less death. True belief is in your heart and soul. Would your pet like to see you so saddened, guilty, and unable to go on? If you had died, would you want your pet to continue having a good, fulfilling life without you?

Regardless of your concern over religion, the important principle in resolution of grief is the strength within yourself. Responsibility is best directed to self now. You can continue to be the wonderful person your pet so loved. Your duty now is to yourself through constructive mourning, releasing of the pain, cherishing the loving memories of your physical life with your pet, and realizing that your pet's physical death has not ended your loving relationship.

DEPRESSION

During your mourning, it seems all that you can focus upon and care about is your pet's death and your own terrible misery. All else in life seems unimportant. Your emotions are overwhelming. You feel numb, indifferent. You may endure a severe sense of loss of internal strength. Each passing hour and day is deeply saddening. Your heart aches, and in deep sorrow you consider that this may be a point of no return. This is depression.

Depression is usually the most difficult stage of your mourning. You may experience a wide range of symptoms, including physical fatigue, feelings of uncaring, loss of ambition and desires, inability to concentrate, detachment from life, the need for solitude, discontentment and avoidance of normal daily activities, and upset of your normal sleep patterns. You may cry frequently, feel listless, and no longer find pleasure in the activities or company of loved ones. There is a void in your life. You may feel that your sense of worth has slipped away. Psychic suffering and despair engulf you, and there seems no way to halt its influence.

Almost everyone experiences depression during life. For most people, it is a brief period of unrest, but for others it can be an intense emotional drowning. In bereavement, depression creeps upon you as an unconscious attempt to numb your pain and make an escape from suffering.

It is common for all of us to withdraw when situations become unbearable and our strong emotions make coping difficult. There may be carelessness for what other people are doing or what is going on around us. In some respects, this is good, because all of your energies need to be safely collected and focused toward your resolution. Feeling negative and abstaining from all that surrounds you are common responses in grief.

Depression is such a powerful response that it suffocates even the strong emotion of guilt. In depression, there is no longer the motivation to feel any emotion. No more shock, disbelief, denial, anger—there is only emptiness in your heart, soul, and mind.

In this abyss of emptiness, you may perceive as invasive and harassing caring friends who lend support and try to help you. You may become annoyed with their efforts because you want to be left alone to mourn. You may even feel that the loss of your pet is too personal and intense to share with those people closest to you. You may wonder how another person could possibly understand your sadness. You construct a barrier of self-protection from outside influence. Your sorrow for your pet and emptiness within yourself stand between you and the rest of the world. You tell yourself nothing matters anymore and that no one in the entire world could understand or truly care.

Fears and resentment that your spiritual beliefs, religion, and humanity's philosophies cannot provide adequate answers of what death is, where your pet has gone at death, or if you will see your pet again only add to your hopelessness and grief. There seems no value to life when needed; concrete answers cannot be found.

In your sadness and dwelling of these thoughts, consider that nature provides the answers you seek. In my many pet losses in life, I too have looked for these answers. Here I share with you a personal philosophy:

> *Whether you enjoy gardening or not, visualize for a moment that you are kneeling on the earth, next to a hole in fertile soil, and in your cupped hands you hold a lily bulb. Visualize yourself gently placing the bulb into the hole and filling in the hole with fertile soil. Let your tears of grief fall upon the newly planted soil. See the first sprout of life grow upward from the soil, then at an awesome rate, it grows to full form, with the most beautiful lily blossom of vibrant orange your eyes have ever*

seen. Take a moment to witness its life and beauty. Then visualize the lily petals falling from the stem one by one, until all have fallen and the lily withers and dies. Nothing is left but bare soil. Dig into the soil with your hands and remove the bulb from the earth. Cup it into your hands. What will happen now if you plant the lily bulb again? It bloomed, then died, but if you plant it into the soil once more, it will live again. This is nature's promise. Nature clearly shows us the cycle of death, birth, and rebirth—but we do not always recognize it.

The lily plant will die, but the life-force within remains and it will live again. Your pet's physical body may have died, but his or her soul lives, and if you cannot accept the concept that your pet will live again, you can at least know that your pet's soul, or spirit, continues.

Your depression can be helped by thinking of nature's examples. In winter, the earth appears dead, but does it not live again and continue?

At conception, the sperm and egg join to produce a living creature, but consider that the soul of the creature is not born of the physical world—it comes from the spiritual world. If it did not, none of us would be unique individuals with our own personality. Without a soul, we might be different-looking individuals because of our genes, but our personality would be the same as everyone else. The core of you, of me, and all living creatures is not of the physical world, but of a spiritual realm that we cannot fully define. A creature can be brain dead, yet the life-force within has not yet given up and left the physical world. Therefore, we can assume that an energy—a life-force—a soul, is what truly makes us exist, and that the physical body is the armor it wears and uses in this world.

Feelings of failure and inadequacy are what make you feel guilt and depression. These feelings can sometimes cause a deep, life-threatening depression. Suicidal feelings are not uncommon in pet grief. It is comforting to note that suicide is usually fantasized in the mind's desire to reunite with the deceased loved one, but it is rarely carried through. It is not common for grieving pet owners to commit suicide or seriously consider it an option to overcome grief. Grieving is only a trigger mechanism for suicidal thoughts in individuals with previous bouts of severe depression or psychological problems—it is not the cause.

If you feel suicidal, get help. Self-destruction and repetitive mental battering is not the answer to your pain. Your pet surely would want you to be happy—to continue living and loving with his or her memory. Remember, your pet's death is not the end of your loving relationship—it is a new beginning. Reach out with love between this physical world and the spiritual world, and continue your bond.

Know that your depression is normal. However, if you suffer continuously and have strong self-destructive thoughts, you must seek a professional mental health practitioner for therapy. There is nothing wrong with this. There are traumatic times in life when we all need a helping hand. You are a strong individual if you get help when you know it is needed. You give yourself a gift of positive action, growth, and resolution in acquiring assistance.

There is no need to seek therapy unless you cannot resolve these feelings on your own. Whether or not it is necessary is best judged by your mental and physical health before your pet's death, and how any problems before affect your ability to cope with your grief.

Talk about your feelings with your family and friends. There is nothing to be ashamed of in admitting your depression could use support. Seek out a support group for pet loss. Speak with your veterinarian, and ask for a referral to a support group or credible bereavement counselor. Give yourself opportunities to have the support, understanding, and tender loving care from those people around you who want to help.

Though a long, grim journey, depression has advantages in its resolution. You have the opportunity to meditate on the upsetting reality suddenly confronting you. Through time devoted to acceptance and meditation, you can gain emotional strength and regain perspective. You will be brought upward from sorrow and have the ambition to go on living. Give yourself time to accept and understand your pet's death and know the transition of your beautiful, loving relationship is not the end.

In later chapters, you will find suggestions for memorializing your pet and constructive actions to help you resolve the emotions presented in this chapter.

Be strong. Have faith in yourself as your pet always has.

✦

Endnotes

1. Sife. *The Loss of a Pet*, p. 24.
2. Ibid., p. 31.
3. Ibid., p. 32.
4. Ibid., p. 46.
5. Ibid., p. 53.

Chapter Three

Bereavement & Children

UNLIKE YOUR RELATIONSHIP WITH YOUR PET, your child and pet have a sibling-like bond. In many households, the family considers their pet a family member. There is nothing unusual about this. When your child is sad, he or she seeks out their best friend and closest companion, their pet. If your child misbehaves and you scold, your child's pet is a friend who will listen to your child's side of the story. When bullies at school tease or torment your child or when he or she feels unable to fit in with peers, a pet provides a friendship of pure acceptance and love, without judgment or criticism. At night, if your child becomes frightened by shadows or monsters in the closest, a trusty pet cuddles and comforts your child to sleep. When you are busy with household chores, your child receives a sense of security and continuity from a pet. Love and trust are learned through your child's growing relationship with a pet.

Your child learns responsibility and gains self-esteem from the bond that develops with their pet. This influences your child's growing personality and attitude in life. In an adult world where your child can be overwhelmed or confused by complicated adult matters, there is a special bond with the shared innocence, freedom, and caring of their pet. Your child's pet is a living symbol of their emotional security.

Your child needs to experience some of the bereavement of pet loss to learn healthy ways of resolution, which will be of benefit later in life. As your child's guide, you need to share in the learning and healing process once your child has realized the feeling of loss and grief.

It is a shame when a child's sadness at the death of a pet is not taken seriously. The emotional turmoil a child feels at a pet's death can be overwhelming. Jokes, humor, and belittling a child's very real emotional upset causes the child more suffering, shame, guilt, pain, and negative emotions.

As adults, we attempt to protect children from grief because we consider it an adult problem that they should not have to endure and deal with. In our hectic schedules of work and home, we can easily trivialize a child's loss and forget to give them the respect, understanding, and loving attention they desperately need. We know that death is emotionally upsetting and that there are no adequate answers to our children's questions about death. In our own grief over pet or human loss, we are upset and struggling emotionally as well.

Regardless of your child's age, sooner or later he or she will be confronted with the experience of death. To parents, the topic of death is as uncomfortable to explain as the birds and the bees lecture. How do you begin to explain? What should your child know or not know? How can you best explain without upsetting your child further?

As parents and adults, we have an obligation to acknowledge our children's knowledge and experience of death in a constructive manner. A child's response to death is more unconditioned and curious than an adult's response. The response will vary from child to child, depending on the age and stage of intellectual development. Often we forget how aware our children are and we try to save them from experiencing emotional pain. Many times parents act as though the death is trivial, although they only have the best interests of their child at heart.

When a human loved one dies, younger children often are not allowed to attend the funeral, wake, and burial. Parents sometimes keep their children from visiting an individual who is dying. They shelter their children from death because they feel that their children are unable to understand or sympathize, or that the reality of death will scare their children, but death is a part of life. There are many situations that are uncomfortable and frightening, but education makes the difference. Children need to be allowed the natural act of mourning.

One reason to give your child education of death and grief is so that he or she can learn to give and receive sympathy as they grow older. Your child eventually will recognize death and define it, and coping can be made easier by having firsthand experiences that provide a healthy, realistic understanding.

Allow your child to experience the natural and very real feelings of death and loss. Be supportive and available to answer your child's curious and heartfelt questions. Remember that your child is very intuitive. Adults sometimes overlook this fact and tend to think that children are too immature intellectually to perceive what is really happening. When adults grieve a death and exclude their children, negative results can occur. Children may wonder why their mom or dad is so sad and crying, or why no one will tell them what is wrong. Your child can feel ashamed, excluded, and guilty at not having your trust in telling him or her why you are upset. Your child knows when you are upset and when he or she is excluded from important family situations.

Don't shy away from crying and grieving if you suddenly feel the familiar twitching of your facial muscles and warmth and swelling of your eyes while your child is around. Children need to be sensitized to other people's emotions.

Your child watches television and sees movies where death—usually violent and without mourners—is introduced. Your child hears about death at school, from friends, and during your conversations when you think your child is not paying attention. If your child is old enough, he or she may recognize that death is not a subject openly talked about. Keep in mind that by excluding your child, he or she may feel guilty or may feel that you consider his or her feelings as somewhat bad behavior. Children may not understand why or how they acted wrongfully to make parents exclude them, and they'll wonder in confusion.

Many pagan adults speak of death to their children to ease their children's mind that rebirth will happen for the pet, or at least that the pet's spirit will continue. If your child is of an age to understand, discuss with him or her theories about what happens at physical death and the afterlife. Education about death and how it is an inevitable part of life can be a positive enlightenment and growth experience. Explaining such philosophy and theory of death to your child needs to be done in a very elementary way, however. For younger children, one idea is to explain the subject through a fairy-tale format. Tell a story that addresses death and involves your spiritual beliefs and deities, such as the Wiccan religion's Goddess aspect of the Crone. The story can help your child understand that death is a part of life and that a Divine Source—a god, goddess, angel, creator— is watching over his or her pet in the afterlife. This provides a suitable education of death and a sense of security for your child that the pet is safe in the afterlife. It also allows your child peace of mind that the pet is with your child in spirit and memory.

Proceed carefully. Hoping your child will forget about a pet's death is unreasonable. Do we as adults truly ever forget? If you avoid discussing the issue, your child may perceive you as betraying trust, which ultimately damages your image in his or her mind. The incident could create feelings of anger, mistrust, resentment, and worry. It is not uncommon for negative childhood experiences, particularly when a child feels greatly wronged, to resurface emotionally later in life.

Also, your avoiding discussion of the issues involved can lead to your child suffering stress and problems in daily activities, or physical and emotional symptoms, such as depression, poor performance in school, misconduct, and nightmares.

If you have a problem coping with death, you will have trouble explaining death to your child in a comfortable and reassuring way. What is reassuring for you is to remember that children are accepting and resilient. What we as adults perceive as unthinkable or horrible may simply be unseen by a child because of their inability to fully understand all components. Of utmost importance is that you do not lie or ignore your child's questions or concerns. If you become upset yourself, explain your feelings. When you are crying over your pet's death and your child questions you about it, take the time to explain. If you do not, your child withdraws and feels as if they might have caused you to be so upset.

Encourage Your Child's Questions

The best way to begin a discussion about death is to ask your child what he or she thinks it is. For example, "Max was sick, and he died. Do you know what that means?" Your child may have a confused understanding or think it is like what happens on cartoon shows, which is unrealistic. Your child may surprise you with a perceptive answer. Base what you say on the answers you receive from your child. Use a simple and straightforward explanation. Your child will then more fully understand the death and know that the feelings of grief are normal and natural.

Reassure your child that his or her feelings are natural, and you are here to help. For example, "I know you hurt and miss Max, but I want you to know that I will help you understand and that I understand your feelings." Work on your child's level by gauging what upsets or confuses him or her regarding their pet's death.

Present answers to your child's questions in a simple way. Do not oversimplify to the point that you tell your child "FiFi went bye-bye on a long trip" or "Jake was sick and had to go away." These are not positive, constructive answers. Your intention may be to protect your child, but when your child grows to realize the truth, it will seem a cruel, betraying, offensive lie.

If your child's pet is diagnosed with a sickness or injury that will result in death, discuss pet death and grief with your child before the pet dies. You may be surprised at the willingness and awareness your child has in discussing the terminal illness or injury and death.

With smaller children, it is easy for adults to become impatient with a child's repetitive statements of "But I want him back" or "Why can't I see him?" Younger children may not be able to intellectually accept death or understand. In their struggle of grief and to understand, they ask repetitive questions. Your patience and gentle explaining is needed.

It is possible that adults who scoff at grieving the loss of a pet may do so because as children they never received compassionate understanding of bereavement. Their parents may have ignored their questions, refused to discuss the subject, or otherwise made death seem trivial or horrible. These children may have grown into insensitive adults who trivialize your grief because they do not understand your feelings or why support is needed. They do not know how to be compassionate toward pet bereavement.

With children, it is often better to avoid morbid details about how the pet died or physical issues of death, such as an autopsy. These facts may frighten your child. If you choose less detail and more simplicity, your child will understand death in a more positive way.

Your child's grief may range from seemingly nonexistent to severe. Parents can be shocked at an unexpected response. If you trivialize your child's grief, you risk sending a powerful message—this is how I would act if you died. Allow your child to sense how you respond and truly feel regarding the pet's death. Your example will provide answers and your child will feel secure and positive. This is the ultimate goal.

As birth is the beginning of life, death is the end of mortal life in which a transition of the soul commences. Explain death with reassurance; it is neither bad nor something to be feared. Acknowledge that death can be extremely upsetting.

As you discuss death with your child, share your positive religious views and spirituality, which can ease the discussion and give your child a feeling of further support. Pagans can talk about nature's cycles of birth, death, and rebirth. Use ideology your child can understand and be comforted by. If your child is religiously taught, there is the chance they might think they did something to cause their pet's death and the gods are punishing them by taking their beloved pet. Spiritual guidance coupled with death education will help your child overcome this misconception. I see nothing wrong with telling a child that their pet is with the God or Goddess or living with angels. Once you begin to explain death and afterlife, it is common for a child to wonder precisely where their pet is and with whom.

Your child will benefit from your example; remember that you are their primary role model. Treat your child's grief seriously. Share your feelings. Care, proceed gently, and answer their questions as best you can. Your discussions of pet loss and death with your child might help in their coping with a human loved one's death in the future.

WHY DO WE HAVE TO PUT OUR PET TO SLEEP?

When your family pet is ill or suffering injury and a decision must be made to apply euthanasia, include older children in the decision-making process. Talking about euthanasia can be painful and upsetting, but it helps to bring forth emotions that may otherwise be suppressed or not understood. Explain why you feel euthanasia is best and share your feelings. A younger child does not necessarily have to sit in on the decision-making, but inform them of where their pet is going and why.

WHERE IS MY PET NOW?

How can we answer such questions when we don't have precise answers—and we know the physical world answers we have may hurt? Our hearts ache when asked because we feel the uncertainty and pain.

When discussing death, children ask many questions about the pet's whereabouts, if the pet is happy being dead, if the God or Goddess takes care of the pet now, and if they will ever see their pet again. When a young child asks this last question, he or she is usually referring to this life. Assess exactly what your child means to provide proper guidance. Avoid answering "I don't know," which leaves your child feeling lost and confused. Although you may not know, try to provide answers that will satisfy the question and ease your child's mind.

Sometimes your child may ask different adults the same questions and get different answers. If this happens, explain that people have different beliefs about death and afterlife, but that this is what you believe to be correct. Although we all have different beliefs, we can agree that death is not an end but a transition. Tell other family members and friends what you have told your child about death and grief.

Your child may disagree with your answer and say, "I think Fluffy is in heaven." But as long as your child has a comforting answer, it is okay to disagree. Accept your child's beliefs and adjust your discussion to include them.

Be aware that in discussions with your child about a pet's death, he or she may misinterpret answers. Some of the common answers and your child's possible interpretations include the following:

✦ *Your pet got sick and died* (without further explanation or if untrue). To your child, if their pet got sick and died, that means everyone close to your child who falls ill might automatically die. This thinking can create a phobia. You need to explain further.

✦ *Your pet went to sleep forever.* Your child might develop a phobia, thinking that sleeping can result in death.

✦ *Your pet ran away from home* (if untrue). Your child can become suspicious if you tell him or her a pet ran away and that is not what happened. Your child may realize you are being dishonest or wait in agony for the pet to return, which creates feelings of exclusion, betrayal, and worry.

✦ *The gods loved your pet so much they wanted your pet back.* Your child may wonder why he or she has not been taken back or will worry that they or loved ones will be snatched away.

✦ *The pet had to be put to sleep because of an illness or injury.* Your child may begin to fear doctors and medical procedures. Imagine an anesthesiologist lifting a gas mask to your child's face and saying, "Now you'll sleep for a time." Children understand things literally. They generally cannot fully understand the use of metaphors.

Constructive Coping for Your Child

You can take action to help ease your child through the painful ordeal of grief. One of the most positive and helpful actions is to have a funeral or burial ceremony for your child's pet. Use the Wiccan and pagan rituals and meditations in Chapter 6 or create your own to soothe your grief and your child's. Help your child understand the transition in their reality of not having their pet physically with them anymore, bringing you both closer in the process. You will strengthen your child by the family's desire to conduct shared rites that will help your child see death as a part of life.

After the funeral or burial ceremony, continue to remember your pet. Encourage joyful reminiscing by looking at photographs of your pet. Tell your child that through remembering their pet and cherishing the special love for him or her, their pet will continue to be a part of their life. Encourage your child to write a letter to their pet. Through this, your child can express grief and tell the pet how much he or she is missed. Make a scrapbook or photo album with your child and include the letters your child writes. To help your child maintain a physical attachment, make a memorial shelf or sanctuary to your pet in your home (see the suggestions in Chapter 6). Your child can visit the memorial and talk openly to their pet; both actions are healthy and positive.

Children sometimes pretend their deceased pet is with them, and who is to say in spirit the pet is not? This action is healthy, beneficial, and helps your child cope.

Use outside resources to gather information about death and dying for your child. Look in the library for children's books available on the subject. Ask your veterinarian to talk with your child about their pet's death. This is especially positive if your child knows their pet died while at the veterinary clinic. The veterinarian can sometimes handle the hard-to-answer questions about what happened. He or she can do so in an informed, educated, and non-shocking manner.

A pet's death can cause emotional problems in even the most well-adjusted child. Your child will look to you and other people of authority for words of wisdom and proper guidance. Inform your child's teacher about the death and ask for advice on guiding your child. If anything, your child's teacher can be notified in case your child suffers some hardships participating in classroom activities or seems troubled. The teacher may even take the opportunity to discuss pets and pet loss to help other children and to increase attention to the subject. Only goodness can evolve from such discussion.

Any constructive talking and action you provide your child increases your child's trust and bond with you. Help your child cope and work on fun, pet-memorializing projects together. These actions reinforce your role as your child's loving guide through emotional trials and triumphs in their young life.

Chapter Four

Pet Loss through Terminal Illness

EVERY LIVING CREATURE IS SUSCEPTIBLE TO terminal illness; in our lives we will know and love many people and animals that will suffer terminal illness. The relentless advance of disease challenges your loving relationship with your pet, and the battle to preserve your pet's life creates emotional and physical demands that are born of love and a spark of hope.

Universal in pet bereavement is the feeling that you have lost control. You feel failure in your responsibility in caring for your pet. You may feel guilt or blame for your pet's disease, but in your heart you know that neither is true— your attempts to conquer your pet's terminal disease are weighed by medical and scientific quests that are not always, and may never be, successful.

Through veterinarian visits, you provide health screening and medical care for your pet, assuming these will defeat disease. When a pet is found to have a terminal illness, you may question why the disease was not discovered earlier and blame the veterinarian. You logically know that cancer and other terminal illnesses are silent killers without early symptoms in many cases. In desperation to save a beloved pet, however, your sensitive emotions may overcome your logical understanding.

The onset of terminal illness often goes unnoticed until the disease has progressed and cannot be controlled. In initial shock, you may feel excessive guilt and disbelief, and as a result, inflict blame. You must consider that the progression of terminal illness in pets is similar to disease in our own species. Our partnership with medical professionals to maintain health and conquer disease does not secure success in prolonging life in ourselves or our pets. Medical research, vaccines, tests, and cures may prolong the quality of life and fight the war of disease, but they are no repellent. Preventative medicine is the only measure we can take to prolong health, vitality, and the life span for ourselves and loved ones.

If your veterinarian informs you of your pet's terminal illness, remember it is a moment of distress for the medical care provider as well. Devoted veterinarians are animal lovers themselves and having to be a messenger of death is agonizing for them. Your veterinarian may feel a sense of failure, guilt, and sorrow. We often have preconceived notions that our health professionals are callused to the point of constructing invisible walls, prohibiting the ability to feel such distress. We can wrongfully consider our physicians as gods to some degree, and expect more of them than can be realistically given.

Love for your pet and the willingness to suffer emotional, psychological, physical, and financial hardship is no competition against an invisible killer. The harsh reality is that blood transfusions, radiation, and other medical action to fight terminal illness does not often result in a cure. Your pet's life may be prolonged, but you may have to accept that no cure exists. Desperation to prolong the life and loving relationship between you and your pet need not become a perpetuated existence of suffering and discomfort. Suffering not only pertains to your pet's quality of life, but your own. It is common for pet lovers to suffer loss of the quality of life through emotional breakdown and financial poverty. You cannot benefit your pet by sustaining their life when the quality of life for you and your pet has dissolved to the point of no recovery.

Your veterinarian may recommend options that can prolong your pet's life with a good chance of a cure or comfortable existence. If your veterinarian cannot offer any hope and options are not available, seek a second opinion but prepare for the possibility that there may be no cure.

The most difficult moments in human life are having the responsibility of deciding whether another living creature lives or dies. Loved ones, human and animal, depend on each of us to make the right decision without hesitation. In family conversations about health and the human quality of life, it is common for an adult to write a living will, or specify whether or not life support should be used in the reality of terminal illness or injury. Our pets are unable to specify their desires, so we can only judge what is best by their behavior, physical condition, and quality of life. Our selfish tendencies in not wanting to be without the love and life of a pet can cause unnecessary and senseless suffering to the pet. We must be cautious that our intentions are to benefit our pets and not ourselves. We can agree that no living creature should be forced to live in pain and suffering. Perhaps the easiest way to determine the best decision is to reverse roles with your pet. If you were suffering the diagnosed terminal illness, what would you prefer family members, including your pet, to decide?

Coping

The day your veterinarian tells you of your pet's terminal illness, inform other family members, especially children. Explain the terminal illness and possible consequences to your children in terms they can understand. It may help to encourage them to speak directly to the veterinarian providing your pet's treatment. Children must be allowed to ask questions and receive sensible answers. Often, their fantasies of what is happening are worse than the reality. Inform children about the illness, not only to prepare them for the coming death, but to warn them that the pet will be unable to play and tolerate interactions. Children need to understand that their pet is very ill and provisions must be made to make the pet comfortable. Although they do not mean to be malicious when they play with pets, sudden grabbing or playing too roughly with a sick pet can result in injury to both pet and child.

Children can be wonderful care providers when notified of another living creature's plight. It is not fair to scold your child for playing with the family pet when your child does not understand why. By being informed, children are able to get a head start in coping with the grieving process.

In family discussion of the pet's terminal illness, it is common for disputes to arise. When medical options are available, the family unit may split. Children and other family members may prefer the pet to remain in the home and to explore other options, even if there is no medical hope. Parents may disagree on proper action. Financial and emotional reasons, coupled with the pet's quality of life, are usually the cause for disagreements.

In talking with your family, let children speak their preference and have their questions answered as best as possible. If you know that there is no medical hope and suggested treatments cannot be financially or otherwise undertaken, explain this to your child. End the discussion on a positive note—reminding your child to cherish and enjoy these moments with your family pet. Perhaps a discussion of death and afterlife can follow, and constructive ways of coping introduced for your family as a whole. (See Chapter 3 for more suggestions on talking to children about death and pet loss.)

If you seek the advice of others, be prepared for differences of opinion. Some pet lovers believe that once a pet is diagnosed with terminal illness, the pet should be relieved of the possibility of suffering. Other pet lovers believe that you should do everything in your power to keep your pet alive, even if it means taking a second mortgage on your home or traveling to an animal medical center thousands of miles away. Remember that each individual has an internal sensing of what limits and degrees of action are appropriate. Never take the advice of another person because you fear judgment or condemnation against your preference or if your instincts tell you it is incorrect. Seeking advice of several individuals can benefit your decision by providing different viewpoints and concerns, especially if you are emotionally distraught and unable to think clearly.

Make a decision you will agree with in the future. As you spend moments with your sick, beloved pet, every second is filled by sorrow. You look into the twinkling eyes of your precious companion, feeling unable to determine the best decision. Any final choice made is correct when based on the essence of love. Through the essence of love, we as humans have the ability to release loved ones from the anguish of pain and suffering. Our ability to make such a decision should be considered a gift of the Gods, not a curse. Nearly every religion is based on love, faith, and charity to fellow living creatures. Prepare yourself for the decision-making through spirituality and faith, and the charity you can provide in love for your pet.

Obsessing

Aside from the hardship of decision-making, obsessing can be the worst torment you endure. The mental monster of obsessing is a self-inflicted preoccupation with your pet's well-being; the idea of losing your pet and your present emotions cause this preoccupation.

Obsession creates a very dismal environment for you and your pet. Obsessing makes it nearly impossible to function in daily activities and responsibilities. There is a constant focus on the undesirable aspects of the situation. This is an obstacle that you need to overcome to enjoy these last moments with your beloved pet and celebrate the physical love between you.

When a guarantee of death presents itself to us in the form of a terminal disease or other life-threatening source, we cannot help but focus on the irreversible consequence. With each passing minute, we are continuously reminded that time is slipping away and is limited. Every moment with your beloved pet is shadowed by the coming loss of life and physical expression of your loving bond.

Time can never be recaptured, and for this reason you need to convince yourself to stop obsessing and celebrate your loving relationship with your pet while there is still time. Let go of the presence of near death and spend free moments exchanging the expressions of love with your pet. Begin a healthy transition for your pet into the afterlife and start yourself upon the difficult pathway of acceptance and grief.

At this time, make your pet's transition comfortable and full of love. Spend as much time together as possible. If you do not let go of obsessive thoughts, you may regret not having focused your thoughts and attention to your pet while he or she was still living. Your intention is better focused on your pet's love, your love for your pet, and enjoying the present time together. Release your mind from obsession and what will be. Your pet is with you now—make this time count.

Celebrating the bounty of love between you and your pet during the remaining time can be enhanced for you both through ritual. Unlike other rituals and meditations described in this book, you conduct the ritual formula in this chapter while your pet is still living. The ritual can best be described as an Initiation rite and a preparation of the transformation of your pet's spirit for the future ascendance to divinity. It celebrates the time when your pet will be free of the pain, suffering, and challenges of physical existence. Blessing your pet through the power and divine love of your deity helps to prepare you both for the transition to come.

Many pagans include their pets, sometimes called familiars, in ritual and discover great joy in sharing faith, love, and sacred practice. If you have not experienced this intimate interaction with your pet in the sacred space of your spiritual and magical practices, you are missing a truly special occasion. The Spiritual Transformation ritual described below allows you to rejoice in this experience. It focuses on you and your pet beneath the celestial realm of the Gods.

Spiritual Transformation Ritual for You and Your Pet

The purpose of this ritual is to gently assist you in enjoying the remaining moments with your pet. Preparation during this type of ritual is on a spiritual level. You need to forget, for a time, the physical preparation and decision-making of possibly choosing euthanasia, making final arrangements, and preparing future action at your pet's death. Now is the time for acceptance, love, and nurturing. Now is the time to come to terms within the higher self and start walking the pathway that crosses the threshold into death with your pet. You begin the transition through balance of emotion, spirit, body, and mind. You and your pet face this divine transition as one in your loving bond.

Ideally, this ritual should be conducted outdoors, surrounded by the bounty of nature, upon the soil of our Mother Earth, and beneath the sky of the Gods and Goddesses. Realistically, this is not always possible—especially if your pet is very ill.

What You'll Need: an altar; items representing the four elements (for an indoor ritual; see the Symbols of the Natural Elements chart); colored cloth (see the color and attribute chart for suggestions); candles; incense (frankincense and myrrh are ideal); a cup of water; and soil (for an outdoor ritual); wand; wine, juice, or another drink of your choice; drinking vessels, one for each participant; a censer for the incense; a large or small cauldron (or a cup); a bowl of salt; anointing oil (I recommend Cypress because it is an oil specifically used for easing losses, healing, and soothing transitions, as well as administering protection to pets.[1] Inhalation of this oil provides an astringent scent of solace, comfort, and strength. You can find this oil at your local health food or New Age store.); a scarf or light cloth (lightweight or sheer and not too large—refer to the color and attribute chart for color suggestions); soft music, if desired, to accompany the ritual

Preparations for an Indoor Ritual: In preparing for the indoor ritual, use the procedures of your religious or magical practice to summon the four elements. The four elements, sometimes referred to as "the four watchtowers," are present to allow the flow of universal energies and protect and guard your ritual work. Capture the natural elements symbolically to acquire an environment similar to the outdoors. Use the chart below to help in the planning.

Symbols of the Natural Elements

Element	Position	Symbol
Air	East	Incense
Water	West	Bowl or cup of water
Fire	South	Candle
Earth	North	Bowl of soil or salt

Capturing each element symbolically brings the natural, universal energies into your sacred space. Through this action, you and your pet activate the powers of nature, the cosmos, and the deities in ritualistic symbols.

I suggest that your sacred space or the area where you will cast your circle be near a window. Whether conducted at night or during the day, the window will allow the brilliance of the sun, symbolic of the God, and the lunar illumination of the moon, symbolic of the Goddess, to enter your home and provide energy through rays of light. Though in daylight the moon cannot always be seen, we know that both the sun and the moon reside together in the sky.

General Preparations: Your circle or constructed sacred space is a product of energy—a construction that can be sensed and physically felt with experience. It is a solid barrier that often represents the Goddess in many pagan religions, such as Wicca. It is symbolic of many spiritual aspects of nature—fertility, eternity, and infinity.

Place an altar in the center of your circle or sacred space. The altar represents the cosmos, universal energies, the earth, yourself, and your spiritual beliefs. Decorate the altar with a colored cloth of your choice and candles. You can mix colors to symbolize many attributes of the ritual and the bond between you and your pet. Your altar cloth, candles, and assorted decorations can be one color that intimately symbolizes your aim of the ritual. You can also blend several colors. The chart below outlines some examples.

Color	Attributes
Rose or red	Love, strength, vitality
White or crystal	Peace, purification, the higher self
Gold or yellow	Divinity, energizes transformation and protects
Silver or gray	Allows receptivity to transformation
Black	Supports transformation and absorbs fears
Brown	Allows connection to nature's energies
Green	Intuition, healing, abundance
Blue	Oneness, calm, perception, wisdom
Purple	Guidance and spiritual transformation

Place the incense, candle, cup of water, and soil at the appropriate element or cardinal point. If you use a cup or a small cauldron, place it at center-left on the altar. If you use a large cauldron, place it on the floor to the left of the altar. The left side of the altar is sacred to the Goddess, and the cauldron is a symbol of Her. Fill the cup or cauldron with water. The scarf or light cloth is a symbol of your pet's gradual ascent through the veil between the physical and spiritual worlds. It is a symbol of the universe or cosmic law. Place it at the front-center on your altar.

No special preparation for your pet is necessary. There is no reason to put your pet through a ritual bathing or grooming. If your pet is too weak to be included in the ritual activity, let him or her stay in a room nearby. Your pet should not be stressed by the ritual activity if he or she is unable to endure it. Sometimes a pet is spooked by the strange scents, your change in voice and gestures, and the unusual ritual furnishings.

Begin to prepare yourself early on the scheduled day. Pamper yourself with a long, relaxing bath to balance your mind and body. Through this trying time, you deserve relaxing moments to tend to your own fragile state of being.

You can dress in a ritual robe, or casual, comfortable clothing. Dress is optional; skyclad is ideal and natural.

This ritual may be performed by yourself, or with other family members or friends. If you include friends or family, plan the ritual with them. Give the participants an opportunity to speak, light the incense, purify the sacred space, and anoint your pet. Participants should dress comfortably and be allowed solitary time for self-preparation.

The ritual script of sacred words is divided between a High Priest and High Priestess. Formulate the wording to accommodate other participants or, if you are by yourself, speak all the words yourself. The outline is a guide; change it to meet your customs or religious practices.

1. Gather the participants and your pet in the designated sacred space. If indoors, shut off telephones and other appliances to avoid interruption.

   If your pet is present, allow him or her to lie where he or she chooses. If your pet wanders the area during the ritual, avoid scolding him or her. Allow your pet to act naturally. Be careful, however, that your pet does not injure himself or herself during the ritual.

   Conduct any circle casting or opening ritual procedure of your own spiritual practice.

2. The High Priestess steps before the altar or in the circle center facing the altar, and states:

   We are gathered on this day to celebrate our loving bond with (pet's name), *as he/she commences the path ever-nearing the threshold into death. He/she walks this path not alone, but is accompanied by an abundance of love, strength, and the eternal presence of us all who cherish him/her.*

3. The Priest approaches the altar, takes the wand in his hand, and points it toward the undraped window (if indoors) or upward to the sky (if outdoors), while stating:

   I invoke the presence of our Lord, that He may descend into this sacred space to both witness and bless this rite held in (pet's name) *honor. May our Lord open the celestial gates into divinity and prepare for the coming of our beloved. Hail O Lord! Father of all creatures great and small!*

4. The Priestess takes the cup or cauldron of water into both hands (or if using a large cauldron, she stands over it with her arms raised to the open window (or sky). She gazes lovingly into the rippling water and says:

I invoke the presence of our Lady, our Goddess as the Crone, that She descend into this sacred space to both witness and bless this rite held in (pet's name) honor. May the Crone eagerly await the coming of our beloved at the threshold between the physical and spiritual worlds as he/she gradually ascends the pathway into afterlife. Hail O Mother Goddess! Mother of all creatures great and small!

5. The Priest kisses the wand and places it back upon the altar. The Priestess kisses the cup or small cauldron and places it back onto the altar (or bows to the large cauldron).

6. The Priest, Priestess, or a participant mixes together the salt and water in one bowl or the cup. That person circles the sacred space once, sprinkling the purifying mixture and ending with a very light, careful sprinkle onto the pet. As this is done, the person speaks the sacred words:

Our beloved (pet name) balances upon the thread between our world and that of the divine spirits. Sorrow fills our hearts, but in sorrow there is great joy in knowing our beloved will soon be free of pain and suffering. In our celebration of the union to come, of our beloved with the Gods, there is the ever-present grief for our loss.

With the salt and water, I purify our sacred space and (pet name)*, in the names of the God and Goddess* (state actual names if desired)*, in preparation and blessing for his/her transition to come.*

After the purification, the person returns the salt and water container to the altar.

7. The Priest, Priestess, or a participant takes the altar or East cardinal point censer into hand and circles the sacred space slowly, waving the flowing incense smoke to purify, while stating:

We embrace the time remaining with our beloved pet in both celebration and grief. Celebration of our beloved's freedom from the plights of physical existence, and grief for the loss of a cherished companion and life-partner in our lives. With this holy incense, I purify the sacred space in which we have gathered to commence the inevitable journey of our beloved.

Once the person circles the sacred space with the incense, he or she places it on the altar or returns to the East cardinal point. You may wave incense smoke over your pet's body, but do not wave it into your pet's face or near his/her head.

8. The Priestess takes the anointing oil and if the pet is present she kneels at the pet's side. If the pet is in another area, the Priestess should go to the pet and anoint one light drop on the top of the pet's head, between the ears, stating:

Our beloved travels upon the star-glittered, lunar train of our Crone's celestial gown. Destined is our beloved for the divinity of Summerland (or heaven)*, where his/her pleasures and wants are eternally granted. Let us not shed tears* *of sorrow and heartache; let us shed tears of happiness and comfort in knowing our beloved will soon be free from illness and pain. Let us not obsess the loss of life and presence, but rejoice now, through affection, the love and bond we eternally share.*

With this anointing oil, I bless (pet name) in the names of the God and Goddess, that you shall enter into the realm of death gently, shedding the physical shell which now ails you. Journey you shall with strength and comfort. Cherished are you now in your physical presence and forever shall you be when transformed into spirit.

When the anointing is done, the Priestess returns the oil vessel to the altar.

9. The Priest picks up the sheer cloth from the altar. If two participants are present, both should grab two corners of the cloth, allowing the cloth to sag so that it almost flows. Walking slowly, so as not to frighten the pet, approach your pet and stand with the fabric held above him or her, stating:

This cloth is symbolic of the veil between the physical and spiritual worlds. Take note of those that cherish you, dearly embrace you in unconditional love, as we walk to the threshold of the worlds at your side. Fear not our beloved, for we will forever be with you in spirit.

10. Lower the veil and softly sweep it over your pet's body. Do not cover your pet entirely with the cloth as it might frighten him or her. The "sweep" is symbolic of your pet's spirit crossing the threshold from physical existence into the afterlife of the spirit world. As you sweep the cloth, speak the following words:

Bound by love, trust, and devotion we step to the gates of the Gods with pleasure and confidence in seeing our beloved (pet name) residing in eternal bliss.

Blessed be our beloved as the veil is drawn for his/her entrance into the realm of the Gods.

The Priest neatly folds the cloth and places it back upon the altar. Observe a moment of personal reflection on the life shared, the fond memories, and precious love.

11. Fill the drinking vessels with your chosen beverage. All participants gather around your pet, if present, or at the altar. The participants hold the drinking vessels high to gesture honor to the Gods and your pet, while stating:

Though the loss of our beloved's presence with us bares sorrow and agony upon our hearts, we know there is not loss, for we shall forever be bound by perfect love. Our separation by physical death is measured by time, and in time we shall be reunited—feasting with the Gods in Summerland (or heaven). Beneath our tearful farewells and aching hearts lies the deepest happiness for our beloved's new life in Spirit. So be it!

All participants drink deeply. The ritual ends, and may be followed by the Cakes and Ale ceremony or feasting if desired. Quiet time spent with your pet is ideal as well.

✦

Endnote

1. Scott Cunningham. *Magical Aromatherapy* (St. Paul, MN: Llewellyn Publications, 1989), p. 82.

Chapter Five

Resolution: The Final Stage

RESOLUTION IS THE UPLIFTING OF YOUR INNER self through positive action. In this final stage of grieving, you are able to release the grief and pain yet retain your pet's loving memory. You are able to heal and take the next step of bringing new harmony into your life. Your attention and emotional focus shifts, allowing you to continue with your life's evolution. Your emotional suffering and pain wane and you form an inner core of hope and self-regeneration. By preserving your beloved pet's memory, you let go of your sorrow.

Resolution has obstacles, however. There are physical reminders (such as your pet's toys) and other associations that you can or cannot escape. These obstacles cause grief to linger because they constantly remind you of your pet's past physical presence. Remove toys and other reminders if these things upset you. Once your grieving has subsided, bring the articles back out into the open.

Another way to help shorten the mourning period is to speak freely about your loss. Releasing the pain makes room for healing; talking about your feelings changes grief into a constructive process.

If your needs during this crucial time are not met, or if you do not complete your mourning, the suffering may continue for years, or a lifetime. When you refrain from the natural process of mourning, you hurt yourself more than the actual mourning. You need to go through the self-repair that occurs in the grieving process. Sharing your feelings with others improves their lives as well as your own and teaches others how to respect and understand the grieving of pet death.

While grieving for your pet, you could be subconsciously suffering from a personal problem or an unresolved, previous death. Depression is a clear sign that more than your pet's grief may be affecting you. If you are unable to overcome depression or resolve your emotions, there may be cause for concern. If you realize this or if a family member or close friend tells you something similar, seek professional therapy to help you cope.

As you come to this final stage of grieving, you let go, accepting the reality of transition and its altering effects. You remember the loving relationship with your pet and continue to feel the intense love. You know that you have physically lost your pet, but you remain with your pet in memory and in spirit. You are able to go on living in a positive light, and your beloved pet warms your way.

The path of grieving is one that you must walk one step at a time. Even people who are attuned to nature find the journey through grief difficult. Healing comes with learning to live with the loss, transition, and loving memories. It takes time to achieve complete resolution. Don't become frustrated with yourself. This frustration can drastically slow or cripple your recovery. What you make of your life now as you pick up the pieces is exercising what you were given by that special bond with your pet, and is the ultimate testimony of your shared love.

Stepping Stones toward Resolution

To improve how you cope with your grief, use the following suggestions, which I call "stepping stones." If you feel emotionally overwhelmed or if some suggestions do not sound right for you, pick those most appealing and do one step a day. Do not force yourself to do any of these suggestions, however; each should be done without resistance. Give yourself time to become ready.

✦ If you must make provisions to have euthanasia administered to your pet, avoid planning the appointment at holidays or on special dates. Avoid the stress and sadness of losing your beloved pet on a special calendar date, such as your birthday or your pet's birthday.

✦ Hold a burial service for your pet, whether at home, at a cemetery, or by cremation. Although a spiritual ceremony is wonderful, it is not necessary. The main idea is to express your inner spiritual values in a loving manner. Use the pagan rituals in Chapter 6 or adapt or alter them. Holding a ritual is beautiful and can create positive and permanent memories. A ceremony allows you to feel a sense of control and offer assistance to your pet as he or she journeys into the afterlife. In house blessings and other magical practice, we help a spirit or lost soul reach the other side; we should show the same caring, loving gesture to our pets.

At the burial or cremation, invite supportive and understanding family and friends. If they wish to be involved in the ceremony, let them speak after you. Include children in the ritual planning and help them carry out the ritual in some way. Sometimes, in such a personal, spiritual relationship, being alone may be best. This stepping stone has proven to be one of the healthiest beginnings of resolution.

✦ If you need to make suitable arrangements and calm down after the initial shock and emotional turmoil, try to assess your employer's probable reaction before asking for time off from work. If he or she is unlikely to be sympathetic to grief for a pet then you might explain the need for time off to take care of personal matters or business that can't be done during off-work hours. If co-workers or your employer notice your distress simply tell them that someone close to you has died. This is the truth. You do not have to reveal any facts. Be assertive, but not confrontational. More than likely your employer will grant you a day or two.

✦ If at all possible, make an appointment to speak with your veterinarian. You may have doubts, questions, and concerns about your pet's death, particularly if you are feeling denial or guilt. Write down your questions and concerns so you do not forget them should you become emotionally unraveled. Do not make this appointment to attack your pet's physician because you are upset or feel the doctor made some mistake. The purpose of the appointment is to ask for advice. If your pet died while in veterinarian care, get the details of what happened. If you do not understand something, bring up the issue and get answers. If the veterinarian is a true animal person and a sensitive doctor, he or she will patiently and thoroughly answer any questions and provide support.

Many people feel put off by their veterinarians. For several reasons, some veterinarians and their staff will not approach a grieving individual until they are sought for advice. First, many people do not wish to talk about death because they feel it is a personal matter. Second, the veterinarian and staff want to appear calm and collected; they want to handle the matter well when you are not. As you fall to pieces emotionally, the veterinarian can ease the process of making arrangements for your pet's body. In most cases, the veterinarian is not truly insensitive—he or she simply waits to be approached by a grieving client.

✦ Whether in the veterinarian's office, at the site of the death, or some days after your pet's death, tell your pet how you love him or her and what you are feeling. It is never too late to express these feelings.

One way to express these feelings is by writing a letter to your pet. Write about your sorrow and include examples of happy memories or silly traits your pet displayed when alive. Writing about your pet's death or listing all the loving memories you have of your pet draws your feelings from within you and objectively places them before you. Recalling on paper your life experience with your pet will be of great value during your mourning and a visible record of your fond memories.

Another writing exercise is to compose a letter to yourself from your pet. What would your pet say to you? How would your pet wish you to go on living and coping? Some people scoff at this idea, but I assure you that writing this type of letter reveals inner truths about yourself. It will also serve as a valued personal document to keep with your pet's belongings.

✦ When at work or out in public, we strive to keep calm and show no emotional strain. At home or in private, however, allow yourself to cry and let your feelings come forth. Suppressing your feelings or denying their existence is harmful and slows your healing process. Also, your feelings may surface in public or at work, where you may feel uncomfortable.

Men especially have a terrible time coping. They are taught to be strong, hide tears, and control themselves at all times. There is absolutely nothing wrong with a man who expresses his emotions, however. Expressing emotions is normal and naturally beautiful. Remember, you need to work through your emotions or they will surface where you least expect—and whether you want them to or not.

✦ Think of a personal way to remember your pet. For a cemetery or home burial, have a grave marker or dedication plaque made in memory of your pet. If your pet is cremated, purchase an urn with a plaque or make a decorative holder for your pet's ashes. Have an artist paint a portrait of your pet to hang in your home in remembrance. Many animal rescue and humane organizations accept donations in a pet's name and often they will place your name and your pet's name on a large appreciation plaque. In donating, you know your love for your pet is being extended toward the well-being and rescue of other animals—future pets that may touch someone's heart as much as your pet touches yours.

✦ Change your entire routine and establish a new one. For instance, at six every morning I awaken to feed my bird and two dogs. I then take my dogs outside. I have a set schedule when my pets are taken outdoors, fed, and can play. Shortly after my cat Louis died, three mornings in a row I placed food in his dish. You have probably established a routine with your pet as well. It can be upsetting to follow the same routine, expecting to see your pet present and then acknowledging the reality.

Get up earlier or later in the morning. If you have coffee and then leave for work, reverse the two. Schedule chores at completely different times. Do not sit frequently on the furnishings where your pet always laid down or came to see you for affection. Rearrange your furniture and decorations. An enormous and emotionally stressful transformation has occurred in your life. Do not cause yourself additional or unnecessary grief by following the same routine with its reminders.

✦ Visit with people. Although you may desire privacy to mourn, visit good friends or date, see family, and talk about your grief with supportive others. If you live alone or feel uncomfortable speaking with family or friends, attend a bereavement support group in your area. Locate one by looking in your phone book under "Mental Health Services" or by calling your veterinarian for a referral.

If you cannot leave your home due to emotional stress, invite people to visit you. If a friend or family member has a pet you especially like or that was your pet's favorite playmate, have the pet visit too. Sometimes another pet who was familiar with your own can provide a sense of physical closeness to your pet and help you to accept the past and look forward to the future. This visit may even be extended to visiting sites you and your beloved pet enjoyed. In this way, you can keep alive and relive your memories without distorting the reality you must now accept.

✦ Buy a spiral notebook or attractive stationery and folder and keep a journal. Record your feelings, both positive and negative. Once you've recorded your feelings each day, never go back and change what you wrote or discard emotional portions about which your viewpoint has now altered. This journal serves as another memorial to your pet and provides insight into your innermost feelings.

✦ Make a scrapbook of your pet with photos, your journal, and your pet's collars, leash, and tags. You will feel stronger, happier, and start healing.

These steps can ease your pain and start you on the path of resolution. A woman I knew made a memorial for her poodle who died of cancer and kept the memorial under her bed. Her husband scoffed at her grief and joked about her keeping her poodle's leather jacket and other belongings. Secretively, she placed all her pet's belongings and many letters of love into a decorative, zippered pillow she made herself. For years the memorial pillow has been under her side of the bed, and she opens it on occasion to enjoy the sweet memories.

My neighbor, a teenage girl, wears her dog's tag on a necklace around her neck. She says one day she will place it in her jewelry box, but not until she is ready.

Each of us has a unique, loving bond with our pets. It is a beautiful act of love to memorialize your pet, no matter what means you choose.

Seeking Counseling

One moment you feel in control and able to handle the psychological tension and agony of grieving. In the next moment you are unable to lift yourself from the dread and emotional pits of mourning. When you or a loved one show no sign of improvement in your emotional state of mind, seek help.

In our modern society, it is difficult to become close to another human being in an unconditional, loving manner. Our pets are often closer to us than other humans. Human personalities and environmental obstacles make it hard to establish meaningful relationships with family members, friends, and co-workers. It is easy to see why some people are dependent and zealously in love with animal companions.

Humanity, however, is striving to help itself. Human beings are expressing a renewed sense of caring and concern for each other—you can see this in the increased bereavement support groups, mental health hotlines, gay rights organizations, feed-the-homeless programs, and many other examples. More and more people are letting go of selfishness and reaching out to help others. Although society experiences many terrible difficulties, there is an evolving, positive public attitude. Individuals are changing how they look at themselves and others.

Pagan spiritualists recognize this change. During conquests toward religious freedom and acceptance in the world, we forget that we succeed in our ways because non-pagans are practicing unselfish listening and consideration. We would still exist and quest toward survival but we wouldn't have evolved as far as we are today without a change in attitude from non-pagans. Followers of other religions are more open-minded, listen to our wisdom, and learn. We have an active exchange of ideology in religious or spiritual practice with other people that once did not exist.

Through this evolved sensitivity toward other people, many health care individuals and mental health practitioners now realize that grieving is valid for one's pet as well as for the death or loss of a beloved human. This acceptance and counseling has become available as the population grows and more households have pets. When you cannot cope, share your grief and find positive counsel. Seeking trained help indicates that you are a strong, mentally healthy individual and recognize when help is needed.

When searching for a bereavement counselor, do so carefully. Unscrupulous individuals enter this industry for financial gain and have little interest in offering true help. Ask for references and talk to the counselor's past clientele, asking if they felt they were helped. This action in itself provides sensitive, sympathetic contacts who can help you in this critical time. You may make new friends in the process. Ask a counselor or therapist for proof of credentials, especially if the practitioner requires a fee for service.

At the end of this book, you'll find a list of centers that provide pet bereavement counseling. If the listed contacts are not convenient, write or call them to ask if they can direct you to a resource in your area.

Spiritual Communication toward Resolution

Resolution is a beautiful stage in the grieving process. Suffering disappears and in its wake comes remembering your pet in physical life and feeling the existing love between you. The beauty of your unique bond with your pet is that the loving relationship does not end at death but changes to a spiritual one. You have your pet with you in the physical world until the glorious reunion in spirit. Your pet's memory and love will bring you happiness for the rest of your life, and then beyond. This is true love.

When I speak of the new spiritual relationship you have with your pet, I describe the love and communication that is possible between you in the physical world and your pet in the spirit world. Many people live by the motto "I must see it to believe it," but it is the hidden realities that are so important to our happiness and lives. Because your pet has physically died does not mean his or her soul, or spirit, does not exist. All living creatures have a soul, or spirit, which continues and is eventually reborn. Your pet exists in spirit and the love between you has not changed. Enjoy the continuing love and your transformed relationship.

No matter your spiritual beliefs in pagan religion, recognize the afterlife and that through ritual work communication with the deceased is possible. Halloween, also known as "Samhain" in many pagan religions, is one occasion when people conduct communication with deceased loved ones. During this communication, there are various ways to talk with and energetically interact in other planes and dimensions with your loved ones, including meditation leading to trance, using the talking board or pendulum board, crystal ball gazing, and many acts of channeling. You can use any of these techniques to effectively communicate with your pet in the spirit world.

Many believe that deceased pets are spiritual ties to the other world and the Goddess. It is common for the deceased pet to remain closely in contact with its loved one, even taking the role of spirit guide for further spiritual growth for both of you. A simple meditation ritual can create a bridge between our physical world and the spiritual world. Experiencing the bridge and meeting your pet can deepen your already existing bond. The loving connection through the bridge of communication is beautiful and empowering as you reach resolution.

Loving Between the Worlds Meditation

Sessions of communication with your pet can be as frequent as you desire and are beautiful exercises of love for both of you. Though different than the physical relationship you experienced before, you will enjoy the energy-based interaction, which maintains its own beauty, sensations, and ways to exchange love.

Your memory of the special, spiritual relationship with your pet can change you as an individual. You may feel like a different person. Through this spiritual dedication to your pet, you may feel a redirection of your life. The joy, learning, and exchange of love and living with your pet has enriched your life and will benefit you forever. His or her love for you, expressed now through bridged communication, strengthens you and helps make you a better individual.

What You'll Need: White flowers, candles, and crystals to decorate your sacred space (these articles are optional; choose decorations you are comfortable with, including your pet's belongings); matches; incense to help obtain a meditative state (sweetgrass is ideal as it is often used to draw spirits); a quiet melody of music; a crystal ball or talking board for telepathic communion

Preparations: Decorate your altar or create a sanctuary for your pet, using the flowers, candles, crystals, and other personal objects.

Dress in ritual robe, formally or casually, or be naked if desired. Comfort is the key.

Darken your private sacred space, using the candles for illumination.

1. Begin by casting your circle or ritually opening your sacred space as you do in your religious practice.

2. Lie flat on your back with your legs bent and your feet on the floor. Relax every part of your body, starting with your feet and ending with your head. Tense and relax

each muscle group to ensure total body relaxation. Repeat if necessary. Feel grounded through the pressure of your feet against the earth. Feel the energy moving upward from your feet, through your entire being, and exiting out the top of your head. You are centered and deeply relaxed.

3. Meditate, allowing your conscious mind to rest as deeper levels of your unconscious mind unfold. Focus your will to the intent of communicating with your beloved pet. When you feel ready, ask your pet to appear to you.

   If you experience a block when attempting to communicate with your pet, ask for his or her help. Draw energy up from the earth, through your feet, and release it through your crown chakra at the top of your head. This will clear your chakras and prompt clarity within your aura.

4. When your pet appears, look at him or her. What does your pet look like? Is your pet in bodily form or energy form? Ask what he or she needs from you. Ask how it is easiest for you to contact him or her. Are there other beings present with your pet, such as other animals or spirit guides? Is there someone else who wishes to come forward to communicate with you? Ask whatever questions you need to at this initial communication. Provide time between each question for your pet to answer. The communication process should be slow-paced.

5. Once you've asked initial questions and communicated with your pet long enough, send love through your aura and say a temporary farewell. Come out of the meditation slowly. Return gently, allowing your conscious mind to awaken.

6. Offer thanks to the gods for making the communication with your beloved pet possible. Close your circle or sacred space. You may want to ground yourself of residual energy by eating. Eat within your sacred space and reflect on your wonderful interaction with your pet.

Chapter Six

Crossing the Bridge & Other Rituals

WICCA AND THE NATURE-REVERING RELIGIONS of paganism have similar rituals for deity worship, celebration of the seasons, handfasting (marriage), and many other rituals recognizing stages of our human lives.

Crossing the Bridge is a death and rebirth ritual that prompts the deceased to cross the bridge between the physical and spiritual worlds. In the spiritual world, he or she may find sanctuary but will be able to return to the physical world as desired. Although the performance of this ritual is different throughout pagan religions, all have the same concept and goal. "Crossing the Bridge" is the term associated with all traditions of contemporary paganism and is meant to be performed for the deceased human loved one. It can be slightly altered, however, to provide ritualistic guidance for your deceased pet.

You'll find several rituals and meditations in this chapter. The Cleansing the Gate ritual symbolically marks the beginning of a new state of existence for your beloved pet from physical existence to spiritual existence. Crossing the Bridge is a ritual that I created for pagans who have solicited my counsel during this time of transformation in their relationship with their beloved pet. Grieving with the Crone and Seven Wheels toward Healing are two meditations that can help release negative feelings as well as prompt healing, emotional stability, balance, and spiritual flow of positive energies.

Deciding on a Ceremony

In thinking about whether or not to have a wake, funeral, or religious death ceremony for your pet, consider what you desire and what you wish to avoid. If you are unable to conduct a ceremony with your family because of opposing religious beliefs, plan a later ceremony for yourself at the burial site, or with friends of like mind.

If your pet is cremated, you can bury his or her cremains or scatter them in a sacred place. Some individuals choose to keep their beloved's ashes inside their home in a decorative urn or container. If your pet is cremated, keeping the ashes allows you to conduct a ceremony at your convenience and with the additional flexibility and privacy that home burial can offer.

These rites, or one that you create, will not rid you of the emotional distress and coping that must accompany grief of your pet's death. The rites are meant to help you recognize, accept, and feel better about the transformation of your life without your pet's physical presence and to assist your pet through his or her transition into the spirit world. Most actions in the rituals are symbolic of nature and each one acts as its own spell to see that your wishes for your pet are done.

Death ceremonies symbolize an end to one stage of your life and the beginning of another. Everything around you seems to have changed—and much of it has. This is the time to be joyous that your pet's soul journeys to heavenly freedom from the struggles of its physical existence.

The Beginning

With every ending, there is a beginning. Like the changing seasons and the cosmos, our lives wax and wane through a universal divine essence. There is no dark, gruesome finale, but rather a bright hope for eternal life in spirit and reunion. Although coping with your pet's death is an emotionally difficult time, it is also a time of change, transformation, and rebirth of self.

In Chapter 2 we discussed what death is, including the definitions of transmigration, transmutation, reincarnation, and forms of rebirth. These theories have significant importance in this chapter because they are the backbone of the rituals and meditations. No matter what your spiritual practice, you have theories and beliefs regarding death and the afterlife that you can exhume during these exercises.

In Chapter 5, you were encouraged to put your pet's belongings into storage for a short time immediately following his or her death. In this chapter, we'll use a ceremony similar to a Wiccan House Blessing to conduct a ritualistic cleansing of your home and the space shared with your pet. This ceremony exerts positive energies and purification of the surroundings, and eases the unexpected transformation. It also begins a cycle of nature to free your pet's spirit toward divinity, peace, and freedom, and allow him or her to pass between the physical world and the spiritual world at any time.

How can such a ritualistic cleansing be helpful? In temporarily cleansing your home of the physical objects and reminders that upset you, you begin the healing cycle of acceptance of change. As you accept the transformation, you begin to heal and realize that your pet's soul is free. His or her soul can unite with the essence of your deities for sanctuary, spiritual freedom, and eventual rebirth.

In performing the rituals, are you casting out your pet's presence in your life? You are not stripping your pet's presence from your life. At this moment, you need to recognize and accept the transformation of your pet's being. By performing these rituals, you mark your understanding and accept that this transformation has already begun and must now be completed. These rituals are healthy exercises and allow you to move through the stages of grief without constant reminders of the physical being and presence your pet once shared with you.

It is time to begin a spiritual and esoteric relationship with your pet.

Cleansing the Gate

Throughout history there have been mythological stories of a gate between our physical existence and the spiritual world. In Greek mythology, this gate exists in Hades, a city named after the son of Crones and Rhea and brother of Zeus and Poseidon. Hades is not hell, it is "the Unseen," the netherworld in which Lord Hades rules. The Greeks gave utmost respect to this Lord of Death and revered him in order to secure the spiritual condition of the departed souls.[1] The Greeks believed that after a proper burial, the deceased arrive at one of the rivers of Hades, Styx or Acheron, where a cloaked being rows them across the Charon. Cerberus, the hound, guards the gate into Hades and protects its souls.

Ancient Egyptians depicted the gate between the physical and spiritual worlds as a ladder that a person must erect on the God Geb (the earth), and climb until reaching the gate within Goddess Nut (the sky). The ladder helped the deceased person ascend to heaven.[2]

The gate symbolizes our efforts to visualize a physical connection between our world and the spiritual world. It provides a sense of passing through the gate in time. It is our life destiny.

The purpose of the Cleansing the Gate ritual is to purify your emotional state, physical realm, and spiritual unconsciousness. As it purifies, it helps you to accept the death, allowing the transformation and beginning the healing process. Many individuals consider this ritualistic activity as a way to help a beloved pet into the awaiting divinity of the gods and oneness. The ritual can be a reassurance that your passing pet's soul will indeed be graced with ease in the spiritual journey toward his or her heavenly destination.

What You'll Need: Storage boxes to temporarily hold your pet's belongings; two vessels or glasses, one filled with salt and the other with water; optional: soothing music, incense, candles and matches.

Preparations: If you live with another individual or with your family, you may ask them to join you in this exercise. If you feel this ritual is too intimate to share, conduct it alone.

Unplug the telephone, draw the shades, and turn off the television and radio. Surround yourself with reassuring privacy and peace. Peace is the necessary ingredient to this exercise.

Feel free to conduct this ritual as ceremonially or casually as you prefer. Alter it to meet your spiritual needs.

1. Vacuum, dust, wash windows, and tidy your living space—especially the areas your beloved pet traveled frequently. Move furniture around to physically alter your living space and redecorate as you wish. There is a change, a transformation, that needs to be recognized, accepted, and adapted to. Physically moving furniture greatly helps this transformation.

2. Leave your pet's belongings where they are for the moment. You may arrange a temporary altar that consists of ritualistic implements you use during your spiritual or magical practice.

   Every religious and magical tradition of paganism has a formula for casting a circle, mixing a purification potion, and other ritual phases. You may choose to incorporate your practice to perform the purification of space or follow my instruction. (For definitions and explanations of ritual tools used, refer to the Glossary.)

3. Set the vessels of salt and water on a table or altar within the room your pet was in most often. Take a few moments to stand before the vessels or sit and meditate.

   During the spiritual cleansing process, you may choose to listen to music, light incense, or burn candles. Ask your deity for compassion and guidance as you cope with the loss of your beloved animal companion. Express aloud to your God or Goddess exactly what you desire for your pet, such as "It is my deepest desire that Sheba be embraced within the nurturing arms of my Goddess Diana and that Diana graciously accept my little one into Her divine realm to exist happily, painlessly, and as divine until I am reunited with her" or "I wish Duke to unite with the Gods and become as one with the cosmic powers of the universe until such a time as he may be granted the renewal of rebirth."

   No matter how lengthy your request, use this time to express those feelings within your heart. If you become upset, allow yourself to cry and release your sorrow. At this moment you are telling your deity you've recognized your pet's death as reality and you now wish to accept it and speak your expectations of your pet's existence as it transforms spiritually. There will be tears and emotional pain, but you are crossing the plains of the earliest stages of grief toward healing.

   When you've spoken your true feelings and wishes, tell yourself "So mote it be" or something similar, such as "It is done." This marks the finale of your worrying and dwelling upon your pet's soul as it journeys. You've told your deity your wishes, and now you know they shall be granted. This is the moment where you invoke your love and trust in your deities to help you cope. The time has come to proceed in life and begin living anew.

4. Take a pinch of salt with your thumb and forefinger. Brush the two fingers together over the water vessel and sprinkle the salt into the water. Place your forefinger into the salt and water and gently stir it. If other people are included in this ritual, have them recite a special poem or speak as they wish as you mix the salt and water.

5. Sprinkle the mixture throughout the room. As you do this, a working partner can recite words of power or a segment of a favorite ritual writing. If you are alone, you may do the same or speak repetitive words such as "With salt and water I do cleanse; through (your pet's name) death his/her new life begins." In stating your pet's name and reciting these words, you ritualistically mark an end to the physical life you shared. You have now accepted that your pet must begin a new life, not necessarily separated from you, but nonetheless a new life.

As you complete the sprinkling of the purifying and cleansing mixture in one room, proceed to the next room. Dash the mixture upon your pet's visible, present belongings. In this way, these toys and belongings are forever preserved in remembrance but are cleansed to symbolically approve your pet's new existence of being.

Do not rush the cleansing. If you become emotionally upset, continue. There is no need to stop simply because you are crying or becoming emotionally unraveled in front of family members or a partner. This is the time to express your feelings. Release your emotions freely. If you are reciting words of power and are unable to continue because you are crying, allow yourself to stop the recital and simply continue the cleansing. If you show sadness and despair, and other individuals present do as well, then this ritual has served a purpose. If individuals present become upset, embrace them. Hug your child lovingly, take hold of your spouse's hand, or embrace your partner. Human beings need to feel and experience the warmth, understanding, and love of each other at death. We need to share and experience these emotions together.

6. Once each room your pet occupied has been cleansed, as well as his or her belongings, place the salt and water vessels on the kitchen counter or a table to await disposal.

   If others are present, join hands to form a circle. Allow each person to speak a farewell or wishes for the departed pet. This is wonderful as a self-help exercise for an entire family. Each member can speak their feelings aloud and intimately share the experience. Encourage young children to say whatever they feel. Keep a compassionate and attentive environment as each person speaks.

   If you are alone, take this moment to speak again if you feel the need. Reflect on the happy, joyous, physical relationship you and your pet shared. Think of the fond memories and how best to go on with your life. Consider how your pet would wish you to live without him or her and make a promise to your pet and yourself to move forward.

Afterward, place your pet's belongings in the boxes. Remind yourself that this storage is temporary—you can bring out the belongings when you have learned to cope with the now spiritual and esoteric relationship you share. When you enter the final stages of grief, you can use a shelf or table in one of the rooms to create a memorial, complete with your pet's belongings, photographs, and more.

Burial and Cremation Funeral Ceremonies

Regardless if your pet is buried at home or a pet cemetery, or cremated at a facility, you can conduct a funeral ceremony. Many psychologists, animal lovers, and pet bereavement counselors see such a ceremony as highly beneficial and healthy. Expressing your sorrow and love and saying farewell to the animal friend whose life filled yours with unconditional love and devotion is normal.

If you plan arrangements at a pet cemetery or crematorium, ask employees if you can view your pet beforehand and hold a wake or funeral ceremony. Unless the staff is callous or insensitive, they should agree to your request. If you are refused, leave and take your pet elsewhere. There is no reason you shouldn't have privacy with your family, friends, and pet before any proceedings. Some facilities and cemeteries, however, may charge an additional fee for this request.

CROSSING THE BRIDGE (PET DEATH ADAPTATION)

Should your pet's final arrangement fall upon the date of a Full Moon, Sabbat, or other holiday prompting religious celebration or reverence, you may conduct this rite within the larger ritual. In ideal surroundings with adequate privacy, begin the rite by casting the circle, setting up your altar, or otherwise erecting your spiritual temple. As in many cases, these sophisticated, ceremonial phases simply are not possible in the short time offered at cemetery and cremation facilities, so we will concentrate on the rite itself.

You can conduct this rite indoors or outdoors; it is ideal for home burial, burial at a pet cemetery, or cremation. I have adapted this Wiccan ceremony to our pet death needs. It is almost entirely intact as performed in Wicca and can be altered to suit any religious practice. Format your own ritual if you wish and freely write your own wording.

What You'll Need: Candles; incense and fireproof container; flowers; a bell or horn; your personal ritual knife/athame; altar (even if the altar is to be visualized); wand (any tree branch of eighteen inches or so will serve well); small bag to carry your ritual tools.

Preparations: Dress in your black robe and adorn yourself with religious jewelry before traveling to the pet cemetery or crematorium. If you wish to wear your robe and adornments only in privacy, carry these belongings in the bag with your tools and change into them at the facility.

Usually there is at least one table in the viewing room where you can set up your temporary altar. Place the candles on the floor or around the room. Light the incense in the fireproof container. No matter nature's season, flowers are always beautiful and symbolic of the beauty of life and rebirth.

If you have chosen a burial at a pet cemetery, your pet may be in his or her casket, inside a closet-like compartment behind closed doors. Usually, an employee opens the casket before you enter. Before beginning the ritual, be certain your pet's body is in the casket; sometimes the grooming your pet receives before being placed in the casket takes longer than expected.

Ask someone from your group to ring the bell or blow the horn at the beginning of the ritual. The speaking parts include the Priestess (either yourself, wife, mother, or daughter), the Priest (either yourself, husband, father, or brother), and All (yourself, family members, friends, and anyone else in attendance). Make necessary adjustments to suit your personal needs.

1. The ritual begins with all present standing within a circle, surrounded by the candles, flowing incense, and flowers. The bell is rung (or the horn blown).

   Bell ringer (or horn blower): *The bell* (or horn) *has been sounded in honor of our beloved* (your pet's name).

   All: *In expressing our love…so be it.*

   Priestess: *Today we, the loved ones of* (pet's name) *have gathered in the Circle.* (Pet's name) *is no longer physically with us, and we all are deeply saddened. We deeply miss our beloved. We call upon our Goddess, The Crone, to help us cope. We must not be sad, for we know birth is destined for death, and the beauty of all life must inevitably wane for a time through transformation of the departed soul. Shall we not smile through tears of joy rather than tears of remorse? Has our beloved's death not been a sign from our divine deity that his/her life's work has been fulfilled? Now through death he/she evolves. No longer are the struggles of surviving, pain, and suffering upon him/her. We shall all be reunited eternally, do not fear. That reunion is much awaited, greatly coveted, and will be a glorious time of celebration.*

Priest: *Present in (pet's name) honor, we send forth blessings and wishes as we help him/her across the Bridge to divinity in the realm of our Gods. The Bridge is eternally present for him/her to return, at any time, as desired to be with us here who so cherish his/her love.*

2. All present who have personal ritual knives should take them into hand. If alone, or if only one person has a ritual knife, that appointed person should take it out and point the tip of the blade in the direction of the deceased pet. If for any reason this cannot be done, or it is unsuitable, the points should be directed at a chosen spot behind the altar to send energies symbolically across the Bridge.

   At this time, each person imagines the deceased, beloved pet appearing as best remembered while alive—healthy, happy, and joyous. Those present who do not have a ritual knife can touch the individuals holding a knife. This concentrates energies of love, joy, and happiness that will be lovingly projected from their bodies, through the athame, and sent through its tip into the beloved pet's body. The sending of energies continues for a few moments. When completed, individuals holding the ritual knife place it on the altar.

Priestess: *The unconditional love, devotion, and happiness you've touched our lives with will never be forgotten. As we know, you will never forget the love, devotion, and happiness we shared with you. When we wish to meet you upon the Bridge, we will do so in our Circle, dreams, and within our hearts. You are forever welcome. We wish you all the love, happiness, and freedom from the restraints of physical existence.*

3. The Priestess or Priest gently takes up the wand. All present take hold of the wand. If necessary, hands can grasp another's hands resting on the wand. The wand tip is pointed toward the deceased pet to channel the united, loving energies. As specified in the wording below, the wand is symbolic of eternal unity more so than to project positive energies. It is symbolic of the bond of love as well. (I have witnessed this ritual portion done with colorful ribbons tied around the many caring hands. Use your creativity to make each phase of this ritual special.)

All: *Love is the Law. Love is the Bond. Forever we shall be bonded in spirit. So mote it be.*

4. The wand is placed upon the altar. All present should embrace in loving compassion, understanding, and unity.

The rite has ended. Individuals may choose to approach your pet to bid farewell and have intimate communion. The remaining time should be spent remembering the deceased pet by speaking of happy and joyous times and memorable moments. In Wiccan religious practice, this includes the Cakes and Ale ceremony of light feasting and merriment. Finally, the ritual activity is brought to a close and the temple or circle is ritualistically closed. Extinguish the candles and put away the decorations. The transformation for your pet and in your life has become complete.

Celtic and Egyptian-Influenced Death Ceremony

Paganism is diverse and includes various religions and practices concerning death. Below is a brief explanation of the death beliefs of the Celtic and Egyptian traditions and the steps of the Lughnasad Death Ceremony, which is suitable for both human and animal loved ones.

The similarities between the oral Celtic traditions and the Egyptian faith are unmistakable.[3] Both religions held sacred doctrines recognizing the soul as eternal and the existence of an afterlife. For these reasons, as well as others, these people buried or cremated the dead with the deceased's life possessions and personal belongings. (This is commonly practiced today where photographs or favorite personal belongings are placed in the casket of a loved one.) The belongings were necessities in the deceased's life and were thought to bring service in the afterlife and help the deceased feel more comfortable upon their journey into the unknown.

As was the Egyptian custom, the Celts also left offerings for their departed.[4] Cups containing milk or various items of food were frequently deposited at sacred sites such as wells, groves, and special stones. This practice included ancestor worship as well as acknowledging and paying homage to the spirits that ensouled these places.[5]

Those familiar with two pagan religious practices of fertility festivals at which the dead are also commemorated—Samhain (Halloween) and Lughnasad (Lammas)—realize these two Sabbats are ideal for remembering and memorializing your deceased loved ones, including pets. Both Sabbats are symbolic of the birth and death of vegetation; our ancestors thought the new season would bring rebirth not only to the earth's bounty but also to the souls of those who had died.

The Lughnasad Death Ceremony can be conducted at any appropriate time. The Sabbat alone has its own ritual structure, which is similar to this death ceremony sharing its name, but the Sabbat concentrates on invoking the Old Ones to bless the farmers and those individuals working in the fields and invokes new life to arise in the field itself.

The Lughnasad Sabbat is August 1 and marks the coming months as summer fades to autumn and the harvest begins in earnest. The rind of the last fruits and the chaff of the grain will be buried in the earth or thrown to the wind as a symbol of the people's intention to return life to the earth from which it was taken.[6] In Lughnasad, the Old Ones are remembered, revered, and appreciated. The celebration of life and the onset of rebirth begins.

In Ireland, the Lughnasad Sabbat also honored the God Lugh in festivals declaring peace and a time of rest and merriment between fruit and grain harvests.

The Samhain Sabbat ritual is indeed the most popular of the ceremonies that remember and appreciate the deceased. We are familiar with All Hallows Eve (also called Halloween and Samhain, among other names). I have not included this familiar ritual here because I have yet to adapt a death ceremony exclusively for funeral proceedings from Samhain's purpose.

Lughnasad, however, demonstrates the Celtic tradition and Egyptian properties that interest people who practice forms of pagan religion other than Wicca. Many pagans are not familiar with the Celtic/Druidic and Egyptian similarities of ceremonies for the dead, nor are they familiar with Lughnasad as the Druidic veneration for the dead, which is a very ancient practice.

In the Lughnasad Sabbat ritual, the dust of labor is symbolically washed away by dipping the hem of the ritual robe into a cauldron of sacred water.[7] In the following adaptation, we will use this symbolism as a gesture of the labor of life your deceased pet endured and now has waned.

The Lughnasad Veneration for the Dead rite, unlike the Crossing the Bridge rite, includes collecting your pet's belongings and burying or cremating them with your pet. This reflects the ancient teachings that the belongings will serve your pet in the afterlife and ease the transition. (Ask your cremation facility if cremating belongings with your pet is possible. Certain laws may prohibit objects in the crematorium for environmental reasons.)

Lughnasad Veneration for the Dead
(Pet Death Adaptation)

This funeral ritual is more ceremonial and requires more preparation than the Wiccan Crossing the Bridge ritual. With a little extra planning, you may conduct this ritual at the pet cemetery or crematorium facility. If your pet's final arrangement does not allow for a sophisticated ceremony, however, consider performing this rite after the actual burial or cremation. Plan your ritual as best you can for your circumstances and emotional state.

What You'll Need: Altar; four green candles (for the quarter points); additional green candles; matches; decorative greens; candle holder (large or small); cauldron (large or small) filled with spring water; fresh flowers; bowl with bread (such as muffins, dinner rolls, or donuts); carafe of red wine or cranberry juice (or any reddened drink); chalices or drinking cups; your beloved pet's belongings; straw, fresh corn ears, or bundles of wheat; incense; soothing music.

Preparations: Before the altar, place an unlit candle inside the candle holder and place the holder next to the cauldron. Decorate the altar with the extra green candles and the decorative greens. Place the four quarter candles, flowers, bowl of bread, carafe of wine, and cups on the altar. Also on the altar, put your pet's belongings, scattered or bundled with straw, among fresh corn ears, or wrapped in a bundle of wheat. In ancient practice, the straw, corn ears, and wheat symbolized the ripening crops—here, they symbolize your pet's rebirth.

Use the incense, appropriate soothing music, and additional environmental enhancers to create a sacred and holy atmosphere. You want to celebrate your pet's transition, not invoke sadness or emotional distress at his/her death.

This rite may be performed alone or with a family, partners, or coven. Adjust the ritual formula to suit your needs. Everyone who participates should dress in ritual robes.

1. Light the quarter point candles and open your sacred space or cast the circle. Your temple is now erected.

2. The pet's owner stands before the altar and raises the bowl of bread upward in invocation of the Gods while stating:

   Old Ones, I stand before you as have those before me, to bury the rinds of the last fruits, and toss the chaff of grain into your celestial wind as a symbol of our intention to return life to that which has ceased. From within my heart I seed your breezes this day and bury my beloved (pet's name) into the fertile soil of the earth.

   (In the case of cremation, substitute the last line with a statement such as "*As his/her soul is eternal to exist among the Gods', I send my beloved to the fiery funeral pyres anciently sacred.*")

3. The pet owner lowers the bowl of bread and places it upon the altar. With hands still wrapped around the bowl's exterior, the pet owner continues:

   Old Ones, here and now; it is my flavor of life to which my beloved pet (pet's name) belongs. The warmth of the world belongs to my beloved pet. Eternally of my heart, my soul, my mind, I embrace my beloved pet. May our spirits be as one.

4. One of the Celebrants steps to the altar, takes the red drink into hand. Lifting it above the altar, he or she states:

Bless this (drink) Old Ones, for it is symbolic of our recognition of (pet's name) as of our blood and our hearts. May our spirits not part in the sting of death, or become separated in the shadows of the afterlife. Old Ones, grant us your blessings. May your blessings find us, bind us, and flow through us as our spirits are one.

The Celebrant fills the cups and passes one to each person present, including him or herself. Everyone drinks. The Celebrant collects the cups and returns them to the altar.

5. Another Celebrant moves the cauldron filled with spring water and the candle which rests in a holder beside it to the center of the circle or sacred space. A third Celebrant takes three fresh flowers from the altar and stands at the cauldron facing the altar, stating:

At this time both our Gods and our beloved deceased are remembered, and peace fills the land in our remembrance. With these blossoming flowers of life, I circle the sacred cauldron thrice symbolic of the achieving of rebirth for our beloved, and binding the spell that is cast for our eternal union in spirit.

(This is an old Irish tradition. The women would walk around the sacred wells three times sunwise in order to obtain a wish or bind a spell. The flowers symbolize the sacrifice they were willing to make to achieve their ends.[8])

The Celebrant holding the flowers walks around the cauldron clockwise and drops one flower into the water, stating:

I honor the Great One, the Mother of Life,
companion of darkness and the Moon,
spirit of the moors and empty hills.[9]
Face us with your blessing and allow us your bounty.

Once again, the Celebrant circles the cauldron and drops the second flower upon the rippling water, stating:

I honor the Great One, our God of the Sun, Lugh,
Lugh of the Long-Hand, the Opener of the Ways.
Lugh, protect the questing soul of our beloved pet with
     your power.
Grant the opening of the heavens for our beloved
     and may he/she be graced with the beauty of your
     sanctuary.

The Celebrant walks around the cauldron for the third and last time and drops the third flower upon the shimmering water, stating:

I invoke the spirit of Life,
     the web of all existence.
Grant us the unquenchable fire of Life;
power be to the barren to ripen.
The Old Ones have harvested our beloved,
with the promise of the sacred feast of rebirth.

The same Celebrant dips the hem of his/her ritual robe or clothing into the sacred water of the cauldron, stating:

Into the waters of life I dip my garment;
      as of the Old Ways.
The dusts of the labor of life are washed away;
our beloved's struggles of life have waned.
Bless him/her as he/she joins you beyond;
refresh his/her soul for rebirth and work yet to come.

6. The pet owner lights the candle in the holder next to the cauldron. He or she gently takes the pet's belongings from the altar and kneels with them cradled in the lap before the lit candle. Other Celebrants may also kneel around the cauldron, or remain standing. The pet owner speaks:

   Old Ones, liven my saddened heart. Hear my voice. I have wept tears of rivers and streams, soothe me.
   I call to you in heart of my beloved (pet's name), *in*
         echoes,
   through the hills of the earth—answer.
   Bathe my beloved in your sacred pools of sanctuary.
   Grant my pet your blessings of growth and rebirth.
   May our souls forever unite in spirit as one.
   Allow my eyes to see the harvest of wheat, then the
         budding of grain...
   through this I will know my beloved lives again.

7. During a silent moment, reflect upon the deceased pet's life, give thanks to the Old Ones who have heard, and project the personal blessings and energies to help your pet's soul on its journey.

8. The pet owner takes the bundle of the pet's belongings and passes them through the incense smoke or the candle smoke or sprinkles them with the sacred water of life

from the cauldron. He or she gently places the belongings next to the pet's body inside the casket or, in the case of cremation, next to the cremains.

9. The pet owner kneels again at the candle before the altar and passes his or her hands through the candle smoke, just above the flame, three times. This gesture is symbolic of the acceptance of the pet's physical death through purification, and warming to the continuing, loving relationship through spirit.

10. Immediately afterward, the pet owner touches his or her palms upon the surface of the cauldron water. Each Celebrant also touches their palms to the sacred cauldron water. All present place their wetted palms over their eyes, so the palms touch the eyelids, and conduct a moment of meditation, farewell to the deceased pet, or reverence to the Gods. This is symbolic of washing the eyes with the waters of life to open the eyes, heart, soul, and mind to recognition of the transition in life, and the insight of rebirth.

The rite has ended. Close the circle and temple according to your spiritual practice. The Cakes and Ale ceremony may follow this rite. Share fond memories of the deceased pet, partake of the breads, and drink. Remove all religious articles from the facility room and clean up. The final arrangements of the deceased pet, such as burial, can now be done, if not completed already.

Rite of Release

The neo-pagan Rite of Release is originally from the "Pagan Way" rituals composed by Ed Fitch.[10] Ed Fitch is a High Priest and founder of Pagan Way, an organization whose rituals have been in widespread use since 1970.[11]

Ed Fitch has a Gardnerian tradition of Witchcraft and Odinism background with a strong belief, as with other pagans, that all sentient beings have a soul and all creatures and life forms are sacred. He wrote the Rite of Release to help animals that were tragically killed on highways or that suffered other terrible deaths. He believes their terrorized souls remain within their corpses and that clairvoyant individuals can visibly identify them. The rite is also for pets that might be so attached to their human loved ones that they are hesitant to cross the threshold into the afterlife from the earth plane.

In this rite, the soul of the deceased animal or pet is assisted across the boundary of death. It is a simple ritual that you can perform anywhere and is especially useful if final arrangements do not allow for a more ceremonial rite.

1. Make the sign of the pentagram with the right hand and the sign of the horns (hand in fist with the index and the pinkie finger raised) with the left hand—symbolic of the Wiccan God. Visualize breathing pure white light in and out, and say aloud a blessing to help the animal's spirit cross over into the Summerland (a sanctuary much like heaven).[12] To the west of the corpse, visualize an open glowing door that leads into the woodlands or a suitable environment for the animal. The animal's

soul is further blessed with encouragement to cross the threshold and is bid farewell.

Meditations

The following meditation exercises can help you emotionally, psychologically, and spiritually each day. They are simple and do not require yoga experience or expertise. Each one takes about an hour—it is essential that you make the necessary time to meditate. No excuses. Notify the people you live with that you need to have one hour of uninterrupted privacy. Disconnect the telephone and turn off the television and radio.

Before beginning either of these meditations, however, you need to focus and quiet your conscious mind with a pre-meditation ritual. This ritual will also prepare your entire subconscious to awaken with action.

PRE-MEDITATION RITUAL

What You'll Need: Incense (sandalwood, myrrh, or frankincense is ideal, but any incense of a flowery, fruity, or light, pleasing aroma is perfect); three candles; matches; drum.

Preparations: For your quiet hour of meditation, choose a room in your home or an area outdoors. Light the incense.

Whether your altar is in this area or not, set up the three candles. If indoors, eliminate all other light sources when lighting the candles.

1. Left to right, the three candles you set up represent the Wiccan Triple Goddess: the Maiden, the Mother, and the Crone. Light the right candle (the Crone) first, then the other two. (Light the Crone's candle first to invoke Her presence at this time of grieving because She reigns death and you need guidance from this aspect of the Goddess.)

2. Take the incense stick or container in hand and stand before the three lit candles. Outline within the air, with the incense smoke, a pentagram and state: *With the banishing pentagram I protect this communion with my Goddess from all dark and negative forces.*

   Although no quarter point candles are lit (you may have them if desired), face each quarter and draw the banishing pentagram into the air, announcing each quarter. Depending on your spiritual and magical tradition, start with either the North or East quarter. Announce the quarter (for example, "*South*") kneel down upon one knee, and hold the incense above your head. Proclaim the quarter's elemental presence and your honor of it, such as stating to the South, "*Fire!*" Repeat for all four quarter points.

3. Walk before the three candles, point the incense carefully toward the floor, and circle the area three times clockwise, where you will be seated. With each clockwise circle, visualize a white ring evolving around the sacred space. You may visualize a warm, banishing ring of fire or different symbolism. These circular outlines create a boundary between you and any negative energies that may invade your sacred space when working. The outlines also separate you from the hustle and

bustle of secular life. After the third circle, place the incense upon the altar next to the three candles or next to you on the floor where you will be seated.

This portion of the ritual is simplified and short because you are not present to pay reverence to the Crone or the elements or to conduct magic. You are present to invoke them for guidance, energies, and presence for the purpose of meditation toward internal healing and coping of your grieving process. The Crone and elements do not need a lengthy ceremonial invitation for this purpose. However, feel free to alter the invocations to your liking. You are the Goddess' child— she will come regardless of the amount of wording you use to invoke Her.

4. Seated before the three candles, breathe inward deeply, pausing momentarily and exhaling slowly. Inhale again deeply, hold for a count of four, and exhale slowly. Continue for a few moments to relax. Allow the aroma of the incense to shift your consciousness, and the silence to bring peace into your mourning. Relax. Clear your conscious mind of worries and daily reminders.

5. If you have a drum, use it now. At this stage of the pre-meditation ritual you are becoming prepared to gradually still the mind, shift consciousness, and reach your inner self. A soft drum beat, like a slow heartbeat, would be ideal during this phase. Close your eyes, breathe in relaxation, and listen to the heartbeat of your drum— BUMPbump, BUMPbump.

Grieving with the Crone Meditation

The purpose of this meditation is to recognize and accept your pet's death and transform your loving relationship. This meditation, unlike the meditation in Chapter 5 of spiritual communication with your pet, is for the purpose of healing yourself and does not include communication with your pet. If you are uncomfortable with this, alter the meditation to suit your personal needs and desires.

Focus on the Third Eye

Whether drumming or not, imagine the rhythm of a heartbeat. Perhaps it is quiet enough to hear your own heartbeat. Listen, and release yourself from worry and emotional turmoil.

Many individuals fail when attempting meditation because they either do not know a technique or use an incorrect technique. To overcome this problem, continue with the relaxation breathing exercise and focus on your third eye, or as known in the Eastern philosophies "the thousand-petal lotus." The third eye is the sixth chakra. By focusing on it you transcend association with your physical self and mental/conscious realizations. Concentrating on the third eye allows you to rise beyond the conscious and subconscious cares of the physical and become aware of truth, or the true, divine source.

1. Seated, keep your head straight and comfortably aligned with shoulders, relaxed and back. Do not let your head tilt forward. Keep your cervical spine (neck) straight.

With your eyes open, look upward. Do not tilt your head back so you can look up to the ceiling or sky, but rather keep your head straight and look with your eyes upward. You only need to gaze upward with your eyes or close them and gaze upward that way. After a moment of rhythmic breathing and focusing on your third eye, you should feel a sense of well-being and outwardness and upwardness. You are soaring above the horizon and concentrating on your higher, spiritual consciousness. You are free from the physical realm.

Meditation preparation using the third eye, or the sixth chakra, is practiced among shamanic healers. In shamanic healing the third eye is related to the sacred Six, the power of the ancestors. Through this chakra, which radiates white to violet light, we can understand the spiritual connection, the web of life, between all sentient beings and souls. Through concentration of the third eye, we invoke the assistance of ancestors who have waited to help us after having fulfilled their own earthly lives. Ancestors and your beloved deceased await your summons. Having focused on the sixth chakra now, help will be granted for you to cross the threshold into the spirit world, enabling you to communicate with the Crone and spiritually connect with your pet.

RELAXATION EXERCISES

1. You can sit or lie down for the meditation; be sure that your spine does not curve, muscles do not tighten, and you are comfortable. If lying down, place a pillow

beneath your lower thighs or knees to keep your spine straight.

2. Breathe. If you have been drumming softly, cease. Allow your arms and hands to lay limp upon your lap. Sit upright and stretch your body. With your arms, reach for the sky and with your legs, stretch them outward like tree roots in search of water. Now, taking your time, do some relaxation exercises to prepare for our meditation.

Let your head carefully fall forward so that your chin touches your chest. Breathe in, count four, then slowly exhale. Lift your head upright.

Leaning your head to the left, tip it as far as possible, being careful not to pull a muscle in the process. Take your right arm and place it behind you with your forearm against your lower back. Hold momentarily. Feel your arm's position helping to lightly stretch and relax your neck and shoulder muscles. Inhale, count four, exhale. Resume your upright position.

Tip your head as far as possible to the right. Take your left arm, place it behind your back with your forearm against your lower back. Carefully stretch. Inhale, count four, exhale. Resume the upright position of your head.

Breathe normally. Allow your head to fall forward, right, back, and left. Do so gently without strain. Repeat, but this time have your head fall to your chest, tip left, falling back, tip right, and upright. Good.

Your muscular relaxation exercises are completed. You should feel wonderfully refreshed with a renewed sense of calm and balance. If not, slowly perform the exercises again until your body and mind feel free from tension.

3. Lift your arms, bent slightly, and your hands approximately fifteen to eighteen inches away from your chest. Stretch out your fingers so that your palms face away from your body. Your fingers and hands should not be rigid or held tensed to keep them equally aligned. Simply face your palms away from you, facing the Triple Goddess candles.

4. Breathe normally and absorb the warmth of the candle flames into your palms. Close your eyes if you'd like. The warmth, so comfortable and secure, is symbolic of the Crone's love and understanding of your sorrow at the death of your beloved pet. Soon the warmth will be absorbed through your hands, down your arms, and collected within your body, providing nurturing heat that loosens your tensed muscles and mind.

THE MEDITATION

A candle's flame or hearth fire has been used for ages as a focal point in meditation and divination. With concentration of your consciousness, this practice can induce a medium-type trance. The spirit of your pet dwells upon other planes that are relatively close to our physical plane of existence, and it is ideal to sit before the Triple Goddess candle flames now and allow the element of fire to weave its spell as you meditate on your beloved pet and silently, through your mind, initiate spiritual communion with your pet. Listen for a familiar whimper, meow, or snort. Do not take this moment to further emotionally distress yourself in desiring your pet's return. Accept the transformed relationship and bond that you share. Know in your heart that you will always be connected to your pet in spirit, and this new relationship offers the celebration of your undying love. Allow yourself to feel connected to the universe, the Crone, and the spirit of your dearly adored pet.

When you feel the time is right, try a shamanic exercise such as the following, using visualization, imagery, and love to seek the unknown realm that your pet exists in spirit and that is free for your entrance.

We have chosen the color indigo and related shades of the color spectrum because practice of colors in healing has long attributed indigo with a slight narcotic agent that will remove fears of the mind and reassure those afraid of the dark.[13] Indigo and blue shades also calm the nervous system to assist our unconscious inner levels to escape imprisonment within our busy, often overly active, conscious mind. Indigo has for a long time been used to open the sixth chakra, the Pineal gland, which exists as a small, pineconeshaped instrument of the brain of all vertebrates having a cranium. Scientifically, the purpose of the Pineal gland is unknown or greatly disputed. Here, we will target it as the third eye, which is why you briefly stimulated it earlier to awaken your awareness of its existence and thereby trigger its function.

1. Open your eyes and gaze at the candle flames. You are safe, secure, and protected. Imagine you are seated within an old, stone cabin in the middle of a shadowy, deserted realm of indigo light. (Some individuals visualize this as an indigo desert with varying shades of deep blue dunes and powder blue particles of sand,

gently riding upon the Crone's breezes at the boundary between our physical existence and the realm of the spirit world.)

Seated before the sacred candle flames of the Crone in a gray stone room, you know that all you need to survive is within this structure. The structure is surrounded by a seemingly limitless indigo desert terrain that is a realm of unknown creatures, journeying spirits, and the domain of our Lady the Crone.

2. Close your eyes and see the stone room you inhabit. Furnish it willingly with your religious and magical implements and all your personal belongings that please you or that you consider absolutely essential. Take as much time as needed.

3. In your mind's imagery, you are suddenly aware of an old-fashioned, latch-closed window that has blown wide open. The powdery blue essence of sand blows inside, showering the stone room with magical, light blue sand. You arise now as your double or astral body. You look down upon your seated physical body which is resting and focusing before the Goddess' candle flames. You locate a door as an exit from the stone structure. As you consider opening it, you may wish to pick up a familiar religious or magical item to carry along if it provides you with the added comfort of feeling protected. Although there is nothing to fear on this plane, you should be comfortable and courageous as you journey to find the Crone. With your implement in hand, you step outside into a sandy, deserted terrain of indigo. Pause and consider how you feel. Do you feel a difference between this plane and the physical plane of daily

existence? Do you feel safe? If you feel frightened, look to the indigo desert and know that you are soothed, safe, and that the Crone is nearby.

4. You begin to walk straight ahead from the stone cabin's doorway. The dim sun peeks through mist and over the dune landscaped horizon. Your footsteps are surprisingly easy when walking through the powdery blue sand. You look straight ahead and continue.

5. You do not need to walk far. Before you, just past a small dune hill, is flickering fire light. A cauldron hangs over the crackling flames. A gray-haired woman of ageless wisdom and timeless vitality leans over the cauldron, gently stirring with an oak staff. She is the Crone. Her long, streaming hair softly waves in the indigo wind. Her hand-sewn robe and shawl flow in the breeze that seems to kindly coax you toward Her.

6. You approach. She notices your presence and ceases stirring Her cauldron. Her wrinkled right hand slowly waves you to approach. Like a mother so happy to have a visit from a grown child, She clasps her hands together against Her lap and a gradual smile projects loving energies—as warm and inviting as the fiery flames beneath the cauldron that interrupt the soothing indigo plane.

7. What would you like to ask the Crone regarding your beloved pet? She stands awaiting your presence, your visit, and Her heart bears Truth of the unknown—the unknown of death. Many individuals ask the Crone why their pet was taken from them, if they will ever unite with their pet, or if their pet is safe. Each of us has

inquiries so intimate we cannot share them with anyone else but the Crone. The answers are most intimate, sincere, and can only be spoken by Her.

One significant factor when speaking to the Crone is that Her words are positive and true in their essence. The Crone is all-knowing, a deity of ceaseless and ageless wisdom who offers only positive aspects to any inquiry. If you feel you have received a negative response from Her, consider if you are speaking your own worries, fears, and unhappiness through Her. Are you convinced that your pet wrongfully died? If so, you might project that belief to your image of the Crone and believe Her wisdom offers the same as an answer. Allow the Crone, the Goddess, to release upon you the positive aspects of your pet's death and help you commence healing.

8. You may stand holding hands with your divine Mother in Her Crone aspect, or you may sit upon the indigo terrain at Her side and become entranced by the crackling, orange-red fiery flames of purity. You can lie on the blue sand beside Her as She gently strokes your hair and helps you cope.

Stay with the Crone as long as you desire. Hear Her words and accept Her wisdom. It is difficult to accept positive answers when we question death or feel so emotionally negative.

9. Before leaving, be certain to request that the Crone show you your beloved pet in spirit. She will coax you over to the enormous cauldron rim to peer inside at the rippling water. The water reflects the red, orange, and yellow light of the fire around it. You gaze, but only see

your own reflection in the black, watery pool. She smiles at you, placing an arm around your shoulders. Together you gaze, then, gradually and wonderfully, your pet's image appears. You are overjoyed. Through the waters of the cauldron your pet's spirit looks back at you with the same loving, devoted, and excited, dancing eyes you remember. Behold your eternal companion. Behold the safety, happiness, and spiritual liveliness of your pet. Think to yourself that no longer will your pet suffer pain or experience the turmoil of survival and physical existence. See your pet as he or she existed in his or her prime—healthy, vibrant, happy and still embracing your undying love.

10. When you've completed gazing and talking with the Crone, give Her an appreciative and loving embrace, then bid farewell. She will watch your departure from Her fire and cauldron.

11. Cross the indigo desert sands and return to your small, stone home. Close the door upon your entrance and replace the religious or magical implement that accompanied your journey. Standing beside your physical body, you look down, knowing the healing process has begun. With the Crone's guidance you will cope and overcome the distress within you. You can come to visit the Crone and see your beloved pet in Her cauldron waters any time you desire.

12. Your astral body steps into your physical shell, and you sit. Taking a few moments to adjust, you slowly open your eyes. You gradually awaken to full consciousness. Momentarily remain seated and reflect upon your journey. Consider the answers of the Crone and how

best to apply them toward self-healing. When you feel the meditation and reflection has been completed, carefully extinguish the Triple Goddess candles, beginning with the Crone candle, and close the session.

You may wish to write the wisdom of the Crone's words and the experience of the journey in a notebook, your "book of rituals," or on sheets of paper. Later, you can read your thoughts if you become overly saddened and depressed through your mourning. The record of your journeys to the Crone may become an intimate, sacred memorial of your unceasing love and spiritual communion with the Goddess and your pet.

SEVEN WHEELS TOWARD HEALING MEDITATION

This second meditation exercise has a ritualistic format that cleanses your aura. It also cleanses and stimulates your chakras toward releasing inner energies to assist with your internal healing.

A dear friend of mine, a High Priestess who lives in New Jersey, has enlightened me greatly in the practice of the healing arts and techniques using the chakras. She has studied the occult sciences for countless years and I consider her one of the wisest practicing healers in the country. This meditation and cleansing exercise was born of her research and sharing of knowledge. The ritual activity has been slightly altered to cleanse emotional distress evolved from grief and stimulate the chakras toward internal healing in the grieving process.

The word *chakra* is a Sanskrit word meaning "wheel"; chakras spin like individual wheels. They spin in relation to the degree of energy in the system of the individual.[14] There are seven major chakras, which were presented to the Western world through fully developed terminology and mapping of the system from the East. Pagans have always worked with energy centers of the body, and the chakra system greatly helps practitioners develop control over them. In this meditation, you will develop control of the seven chakras for healing necessary in grief.

Within the Eastern texts, the chakras are illustrated in beautiful images of lotus flowers. Flowers are an evocative analogy for the chakras as they can be closed, in bud, open, or blossoming, depending on whether they are active or dormant.[15] You will be using the seven classical chakra centers most popularly taught by yoga.

Physical illness, emotional distress, and daily stress can disrupt the chakras and cause physical and psychosomatic symptoms. Through meditation, you can cleanse, stimulate, and balance the chakras toward healing your distress from grief. The following exercise restores balance to the chakras and develops their energies which in turn benefit you physically, emotionally, and intellectually as you strive to cope with your pet's death.

Chakras represent a complex system for spiritual development beyond what is covered in this book. The information and literary achievements focusing on the chakras and their uses are extensive. (See the Suggested Reading section for several excellent sources for your study.)

This particular meditation focuses on you—your need to cope, heal, and resume secular life—and targets healing within your body and mind to regain stamina to go on. Often we lack the desire and strength to care for ourselves at this trying time in our lives because we are so devastated by the loss. Through grieving you must take moments to consider your well-being, both physical and psychological. As your pet makes his or her transformation into a new state of being, so must you.

Use this meditation as frequently as you require. Many individuals find that twice a week helps considerably, while others feel daily practice is needed. Formulate a meditation schedule that you feel will work best for you. There is no right or wrong pattern of meditation.

What You'll Need: Comfortable robe; pillow; incense; scented lotion or essential oil.

Preparations: For this meditation exercise, you will need only privacy, silence, and a comfortable robe to wear. If you will not be interrupted, work this exercise skyclad to free your body from the itches, restraints, and fidgeting that clothing can cause during a meditation session. This includes jewelry and other accessories that may result in discomfort or prevent physical relaxation.

Select a plump pillow to sit on. If you want, burn some pleasantly scented incense. Native American medicine herbs, such as sage, are ideal to assist the healing medicine you need at this time. Apply the scented lotion or anoint yourself at pressure points (wrist, neck, ankles, and the back of your head) with the oil. You will want to combine the benefits of aromatherapy and natural herbal incense to this session.

No music should be played. Instruments for visual stimulation (such as candles and statues) are not necessary unless you so desire.

1. Toss your pillow on the floor and gently seat yourself. Cross your legs or sit with them in a way that is most comfortable. If sitting is not ideal, arrange several pillows and lie on the floor. Do not lie on a bed or couch because you could fall asleep. You want to isolate yourself from secular activity and reach deep within to the center of your energy for stimulation toward healing. Sitting or lying down in an unusual place, like the floor, helps to acquire a unique frame of mind.

2. Focus on your breathing. Breathe correctly, through your chest and abdomen. Allow your chest and abdomen to expand fully as you inhale deeply. There is no need to tighten muscles when you exhale. Allow your muscles to contract naturally. To develop rhythmic breathing for relaxation, calming of the body, and acquiring focus of your mind, inhale and hold your breath for a count of four, then slowly exhale to a count of four. Fill your lungs, taking pleasure in inhaling the sweet oxygen of life, then release the carbon dioxide slowly. This concentrated breathing is often termed centering. You should practice first, then conduct centering throughout this session.

3. Within your mind, identify your three selves: your conscious mind (which feels your emotional responses to your pet's death), your inner child (who likes to

reminisce of the good times spent with your pet), and your higher self of spiritual beliefs and intent. Identify the trinity and connect the three. Bring them to full awareness in your mind to weave together openly. Give momentary attention to each—appreciating them separately and loving yourself in all aspects as your pet unconditionally does.

4. Visualize an egg-shaped oval of light that surrounds your entire being. Examine this oval of light carefully to search for tears, cracks, thoughtforms, or negative abnormalities. Focus on each thoughtform that presents itself. Thank each, and let go. Releasing these as they surface greatly helps to diminsh concerns, thoughts, and ideas of the conscious mind that interrupt a meditative state of mind.

   Be certain your spine is in straight formation whether you're sitting or lying down. Keeping a straight spine is most important as we begin working with the chakras.

5. Visualize a trap door at the bottom of the egg-shaped aura and one at the top. Open each trap door visually and notice that both have a mesh-like screening so that no low or negative vibrations can enter—only high or positive vibrations are pure enough to penetrate the fine mesh screening. The screening also filters psychic debris and rids your aura of their presence. Concentrate and visualize particles of dirt or debris, representing negativity, trauma, and emotional distress, being freed from your being. Mentally push these unwanted particles upward and out through the top trap door. Continue until all the debris is gone and you feel cleansed.

6. From the bottom trap door, sense the gravity that draws your being on the earth. Feel the earth's energies alive and healing. Draw these energies of the Earth Mother in the form of warm, golden light that floods the interior of your aura. You may visualize this as your presence inside the oval-shaped bubble of your aura and the golden light flooding it just as water is poured into and contained in a glass. You can also use an alternative combination of colors, lavender followed by silver, instead of golden light. Use your intuition.

   Continue drawing the energies, imagining them streaming upward from the roots and caverns of the molten core of the earth. The stream of energies brings renewal, clarity of mind, and healing benefits of positive, natural energies. Absorb the energy and push it downward—sending it back to the core of the earth. This procedure is typically termed *grounding* and cleanses, balances, and stimulates the energies within your aura.

7. After a few moments, draw a pearlescent white light energy from the top trap door. This is the plasma of the universe. Allow it to flood your aura and surround your being in the same manner as with the golden light of the Earth Mother energies. Once it fills your aura completely, release it through the bottom trap door, in the colors of rose or green light, down into the depths of the Earth Mother. (Do not use another color or type of universal energy from the top trap door. Doing so might short-circuit your chakra system and cause unwanted eruptions of energies within each or all of the chakras. All color is a physical manifestation of energy and the vibratory rate of light is determined and differentiated

by the color ray.) Once this phase is complete, you will cleanse the chakras individually.

Chakra Color and Bodily Location
The chart below illustrates the location of chakras within the body and the color used to represent them in all applications of magical, meditational, and healing procedures. Use this chart to navigate appropriately as we continue.

Chakra	Color	Location
First	Red	the base of the spine, coccyx, between the legs
Second	Orange	below the navel, in line with the sacrum
Third	Yellow	the solar plexus; stomach area
Fourth	Green	the middle of the chest; the thymus/heart
Fifth	Blue	the throat/thyroid
Sixth	Indigo/Violet	the pineal gland; between the brows and above the eyes.
Seventh	Violet/White	the crown; the top of the head/pituitary gland

8. Using the universal energies from the top trap door and releasing them through the bottom trap door to the earth begins the turning of each chakra like small spoked wheels. Using the chart, identify each chakra turning and its correct color. Visualize yourself with a soft, plush cloth, gingerly wiping each chakra. Wipe in a clockwise motion as this is the direction a chakra

should spin. Continue until each chakra has been sufficiently cleansed and stimulated. Each one is now vibrant with the brilliance of its natural color and spinning strong. Push all debris and negative particles removed from this cleansing upward through the top trap door where it will be converted and neutralized into new universal energy.

9. Call upon your deity to lend power to assist you. Choose a specific aspect of your God or Goddess that suits your purpose of working toward healing. In the case of pet death, I recommend invoking the power and wisdom of the Goddess' aspect of the Crone. Through the Crone you will receive special healing properties concerning healing and coping through the process of mourning. Her qualities, such as love, passion, clarity of death, and caring for the deceased will be most helpful in dispelling your worries, emotional distress, and bereavement.

   Any deity that you work intimately with in your spiritual practice is ideal. Every religious mythology and ideology has one or more deity that can offer exceptional benefits to a healing session focused on death and grief.

10. Focus on your deity and continue to visualize yourself within your egg-shaped sphere with chakras cleansed and spinning vibrantly. Draw in the Earth Mother energy that is contained within your root, the first chakra. Bring down from your crown the universal energies, the seventh chakra. Invoke your personal energy through the solar plexus, the third chakra. Blend the three types of energy.

11. Slightly bend your arms and lift your hands upward; face your palms away from your body. Within the egg-shaped

sphere of your aura, take the combined three energies into your palms, which are energy vortexes spinning on each of your palms and are called *lesser chakras*. Visualize the combined energy as a mixture of pearl-white light of universal energies, golden light of Earth Mother energy, and yellow light of your personal energy coming forth from the solar plexus, the third chakra.

By taking the energies into your palms, you push out your magical healing energy and power into the physical plane for manifestation. This helps your emotional distress, mourning process, and needs within your physical existence.

12. Concentrate and feel the combined power leaving your palms and slowly filling the interior of your aura. You have successfully cleansed the most important energy centers in your body, the chakras. With the incorporation of both universal energies and Earth Mother energy, you have charged the chakras to healthy renewal, providing balance to your physical body and clarity to your mind.

13. With one final, strong release directed into your aura, create and visualize an explosion of energy that will direct the power to the astral and physical plane for your benefit. Push all of your energy down through your arms to exit your palms and in doing so combine your will, desire, emotion, concentration, visualization, and every ounce of both physical and spiritual energy.

Just as in magical workings, think of the beneficial energies and healing that is taking place now—in the present tense. Will it, desire it, and bring the healing effects into being.

14. Keep your palm chakras open and receive the output of energies back through your palms, into your body, and feel them being re-absorbed into your solar plexus, the third chakra. Visualize the streaming, glowing energies entering your palms, and feel the warmth and strength they deliver once contained within your solar plexus.

    Remember the wise words "as above, so below"? This is the concept here. Both your subjective and objective universe are receiving the blast of powerful, healing energy to give you the needed extra strength to cope and internally heal.

15. An excess of energy may exist that should be grounded back into the earth. Reposition yourself so you are on your knees, squatting down until you can touch your forehead to the ground; place both palms on the ground as well. Rest in this position briefly, then resume your previous position. The grounding is done.

16. Rest your arms on your lap. Breathe deeply, following the breathing exercises recommended at the beginning of this meditation session. As you inhale, feel the renewal of positive energy fill your nostrils and lungs. Many individuals claim the air feels particularly chilly when the first inhale is done, while others claim it smells wonderfully pure and fresh. These are signs that the procedure worked and the energies now existing in your aura and within you have combined properly. Momentarily rest. Energy play is tiring work and you should pause to feel the energies surrounding you. Feel good and know they will help you cope and heal through this difficult time.

17. Thank your God or Goddess and the universal and Earth Mother energies.

18. Visualize the egg-shaped oval light becoming less and less visible as it descends back into your body and chemistry. Gradually, your aura returns to its normal place within your being where it remains until brought forth again for another healing or magical and ritual working. Separate the trinity of selves. Identify each separately, feeling their rejuvenation and renewed energy levels, then absorb these aspects into your mind. Stretch your body and resume normal breathing. Sit and allow your chemistry, muscles, and energy to adjust. Your conscious mind will resume its usual thoughtforms and demand of attention. Gradually come forth from the session, then close the session.

Creating a Memorial

Planning your pet's funeral proceedings and meditating to cope with your grief prompt resolution toward becoming emotionally and physically balanced. Your tears of sorrow become peaceful acceptance, understanding, and eternal love for your pet. Your peacefulness is now a tool for your resolution and continuation through life.

You also regain stamina and begin to feel strong again. You remember that your pet's belongings are stored away. You feel the desire to bring your pet's belongings out of storage to memorialize him or her.

Following are some ideas for making a memorial shelf and creating memorial spaces within your home. In crafting a shelf or planning a memorial section within a bookcase or on a table, you express your undying love and realize that your life must continue in the memory and spiritual relationship of your pet.

Look for spaces within your home to display your pet's belongings. Clear out a bottom shelf in a glass-encased china cabinet and place your pet's belongings there, with photos and memorabilia. Clear off and dust a decorative shelf hanging in your living room or dining room and display your pet's photo, favorite toys, or his or her cremation urn (should you choose that final arrangement).

Many people prefer that their pet's memorial shelf or space be within their bedroom so they can speak to their beloved pet at night or have privacy with their pet's spirit whenever desired. Others choose a room in their home that their pet occupied, where it enjoyed sitting in the sun, or played with the children. If you have children, allow them to choose the memorial location.

Deciding what favorite toys, photos, and items will be displayed is healthy for children as well as adults. Looking through your pet's belongings reminds you that he or she is with you in spirit and always accessible for you through memory. Whether you choose to purchase a furnishing for your pet's memorabilia or construct one, this gesture makes you feel good emotionally and preserves the physical love you shared with your pet.

Memorializing your pet is not silly, though some insensitive people might think so. In my living room, I have a small, wooden shelf that holds photos of my two beloved cats and the urn where one cat's cremains rest. (Why only one urn? Lester, my female cat, was tragically killed and her body was not in any condition for burial. It was more dignified and less traumatic for me emotionally to have her cremated. Louis, my male cat, adored the grape vines behind our home and it seemed suitable and dignified for him to be buried beneath them.)

I stained my shelf a walnut shade and left it unpainted. Some people paint only their pet's name and meaningful symbols on their shelf. I saw an attractive shelf that had the pet's name painted in large letters in the center and each family member's name around it in smaller lettering and different colors—it looks very charming and the children loved the idea.

✦

Endnotes

1. Michael Stapleton. *The Illustrated Dictionary of Greek and Roman Mythology* (New York: Peter Bedrick Books, 1986), p. 87.

2. Ellen Cannon Reed. *Invocation of the Gods* (St. Paul, MN: Llewellyn Publications, 1992), p. 214.

3. Murray Hope. *Practical Celtic Magic* (London: The Aquarian Press, 1987), p. 128.

4. Ibid.

5. Ibid.

6. Dan and Pauline Campanelli. *Circles, Groves & Sanctuaries: Sacred Spaces of Today's Pagans* (St. Paul, MN: Llewellyn Publications, 1992), p. 47.

7. Ibid., p. 47.

8. Ibid., p. 48.

9. Ibid., p. 48 (first three lines in quotation).

10. Rosemary Ellen Guiley. *The Encyclopedia of Witches and Witchcraft* (New York: Facts on File, 1989), pp. 126, 282.

11. Ibid.

12. Ibid.

13. Raymond Buckland. *Buckland's Complete Book of Witchcraft* (St. Paul, MN: Llewellyn Publications, 1986), p. 196.

14. Vivienne O'Regan. *The Pillar of Isis* (London: Aquarian/Thorsons, 1992), p. 57.

15. Ibid.

Chapter Seven

Deciding Final Arrangements

ONE OF THE MOST DIFFICULT RESPONSIBILITIES of pet ownership is making the decision of final arrangements for your pet. There are many options available and this chapter explains them so you can make a rational and suitable decision. The more knowledge you have about the entire process, beginning with where your pet's body will be held while you make a decision, the more insightful and positive decision you can make for the love of your pet and yourself.

Consider what you would want for your pet in the event of his or her death. This pre-planning not only allows you to grieve without additional stress, but also saves you from self-recrimination should you make a quick, inappropriate decision at the moment of emotional turmoil. When you have chosen an option that appeals to you, you can make the arrangements and bring your pet's body to rest right away.

If you are unprepared for your pet's death and are asked to make a decision about final arrangements, try to delay your answer for a few hours. Talk with your veterinarian or a trusted animal-lover friend and ask for their feelings, knowledge, and guidance. You know your spiritual beliefs and your beloved pet; you must consider your own feelings in the decision-making process. The rational and best decision must be made by you, from within your heart and soul.

The Veterinarian Visit

If your pet has been ill and under veterinarian supervision, died suddenly from unknown causes or due to terminal illness or injury, or was euthanized, you will most likely conduct the discussion of death and final arrangements with your veterinarian in his or her office.

In some cases, however, your veterinarian will not explain all your options. This is troubling to many pet owners who need the support and explanation in order to make appropriate, personal arrangements. Often the veterinarian is under the assumption that the pet owner has already considered available options, but there are rare cases where veterinarians simply neglect to inform pet owners of such options.

When you take your pet to your veterinarian's office, the technician or veterinarian will give you a form that outlines final arrangement options. You will be asked to check off the option you desire and sign the sheet. If you are not presented with this form, ask for it. It must be completed and should be completed by you. Often the veterinarian will complete it out of kindness, to alleviate you from additional stress. If you do not choose a final arrangement from the option form or specify your wishes, then group cremation will be chosen for you automatically.

YOUR PET "ON HOLD" AT THE CLINIC

When a pet dies at a veterinary clinic or shelter, technicians place the pet's body in a freezer compartment until the owner decides on final arrangements. Usually, the freezer is large and contains shelves for the pet's body. It is clean and organized. Although you cannot examine the freezer compartment, rest assured that your pet is being handled with respect and proper treatment.

Before your pet is placed in the freezer, tags and other identification are carefully recorded and attached to his or her body. There is no need to be overly concerned that your pet will be "lost" or misdirected. If you are at all concerned that your pet may be lost or not identified, telephone or visit your veterinarian and request that an employee go inside the freezer and check for you. Any caring and understanding employee will be more than happy to do so.

The freezer preserves the body until a truck arrives from a state-approved cemetery or crematorium to pick up your pet for burial or cremation (or until you decide to take it home for burial).

Many pet owners cringe in horror at the thought of their beloved pet's body frozen and in a dark compartment with other pets, but storing your pet's body in the freezer is a necessary step to preserve the body so you can take the needed time for decision-making. Veterinarians in every state are bound by law to hold a deceased pet's body in a freezer for a specified time.

If you decide to pick up your pet, he or she will be defrosted in a holding area at room temperature. Your pet's body will not be damaged or mishandled through this process.

If the cemetery or crematorium is picking up your pet, your pet will remain frozen and hand-placed into the freezer compartment of a truck for transportation.

Cremation

GROUP CREMATION

Negative feelings toward group cremation stem from a lack of education about the process and why it is an option. Group cremation is not unpleasant; it differs from individual cremation only in that more than one animal is cremated at a time. The animals or pets are handled in much the same manner as in individual cremation procedures.

Group cremation is a legitimate option that veterinary hospitals or animal centers choose when pet owners make no other arrangements. Many caring, loving, and mourning pet owners choose group cremation because they cannot cope with the emotional distress in viewing their deceased pet. In some cases, the expense of burial or individual cremation is financially prohibitive. Veterinarian staff, however, will not choose group cremation without your knowledge. Only at a shelter or clinic where stray animals or abandoned pets are on hold will the choice be automatic.

Group cremation is a needed and respected option. There is no shady practice with this process, which is contrary to many people's belief. All phases and record-keeping are done appropriately. Each state has designated, state-approved crematoriums that are carefully inspected.

If you choose this option for your pet, your veterinarian will keep careful records to identify your pet and will notify a crematorium. Your pet will be on hold at your veterinary clinic until picked up by the crematorium's freezer truck on scheduled pick-up days. The truck will probably make several scheduled stops and then return to the crematorium facility. Crematorium employees take the deceased pets from the vehicle and record their identity. They place the pets on a clean platform where they await group cremation inside the facility.

Group cremation is exactly as the term suggests. The pets are placed side-by-side into enormous fireproof trays and slid into large crematorium ovens. The cremation is performed and, depending on your state's regulations, the ashes will be either scattered at the crematorium's property or taken to a landfill. Ask your veterinarian about your state's regulations.

There are two differences between group cremation and individual cremation. First, in group cremation your pet shares his or her tray with other pets. Second, you will be unable to receive your pet's ashes.

Individual Cremation

Many pet owners desire cremation but are nervous their pet may accidentally or purposely be cremated with other pets. This fear comes from hearing or reading about crematoriums run by greedy, untrustworthy, unscrupulous individuals. Such occurrences are rare, however, and there are things you can do to ensure your chosen crematorium is reputable.

When looking for a crematorium, ask your veterinarian for a referral. Visit a crematorium and ask for a tour and a list of their services. Also ask for references from pet owners who have used their services. Contact state agencies or the Better Business Bureau to find out if a crematorium has ever been fined or accused of malpractice.

If your pet is being held at your veterinary clinic, tell your veterinarian that you want your pet cremated. The staff will take care of notifying the establishment you choose or the crematorium the clinic uses, and arrange for your pet's transportation. Sometimes the veterinarian will provide the establishment with your telephone number and someone will call you to discuss the process. Your veterinarian can also act as your medium and handle the entire arrangement if you desire.

If your pet died at home, take your pet to be placed on hold at the nearest veterinary clinic and telephone the pet cemetery or crematorium yourself to make arrangements. Other options are to have the crematorium pick up your pet from your home or take your pet personally to the facility and make the appropriate arrangements in person. In some cases, a veterinariy clinic, humane society, or pet cemetery operates its own crematorium.

Individual cremation fees are determined by your pet's weight and size. Each crematorium has a different fee and deciding factors. Cremation is less expensive than burial in a pet cemetery, however.

Some crematoriums allow you to spend a private moment with your pet before cremation, remain at the facility during the cremation, and receive your pet's ashes immediately. There is usually a fee for this service (often called "witnessing"), but it is well worth it if you are worried about the procedure. The additional cost is due to the time set aside for you and your pet exclusively and to conduct the cremation at your convenience.

Numerous people have asked me, "If I do not witness the cremation, could they lose my pet or give me the wrong ashes?" The truth is difficult to guarantee. Research the pet cemeteries and crematoriums you are interested in. It probably will make no difference if you are present or not; the procedure is the same regardless. Do not feel you must or should be present. Cremation is a lengthy process and is emotionally stressful.

Individual cremation is conducted by placing your pet's body upon his or her personal tray before putting it into the crematorium oven. The furnace operators keep detailed records of where each pet is placed to ensure the ashes you receive are definitely your pet's.

The cremation itself takes approximately forty-five minutes. The oven produces heat that burns white hot; there are no flames of fire typically thought to exist during cremation. The ovens operate at a much hotter temperature and the result is white heat. After the cremation, your pet is removed. His or her skeleton rests upon the tray.

It is a myth that the extreme heat from the cremation causes the body to suddenly ignite and burst, leaving only ashes behind. The cremation itself does not produce ashes. What results is the skeleton, even if not perfectly intact.

A pet's skeleton can sometimes provide clues to an undiagnosed death. A skeleton that has green portions of bone provides evidence of cancer; the green shows where the cancer attacked.

Although this fact may be uncomfortable to consider, the ashes of both animals and people are produced by grinding the bones through machinery that is meticulously cleaned after each use. This is the final step, and it is conducted with care and respect.

Burial

Many individuals choose burial because they like knowing that their beloved pet is resting within Mother Earth and that they can memorialize and visit the burial site. Since the beginning of time, people have practiced interment; it is probable that even prehistoric societies buried their dead. Many graphic records exist from classical Egyptian times, showing hieroglyphic writing that contains mummified dogs and cats.[1]

Pet cemeteries exist worldwide, but most of them can be found in the United States. Most are beautifully landscaped, legitimate, spacious, and well cared for. Many have special provisions that guarantee the land will only be used as a pet cemetery. (When you decide on a cemetery, ask the staff to provide a copy of their legal papers or deed that states the land can never be sold for a purpose other than a cemetery.)

The expense for burial through a pet cemetery varies. Usually the cost begins at about two hundred dollars and increases, depending on the burial plot, casket, grave marker, and other details.

Many humane societies and pet cemeteries offer community burial as a less expensive option. This should not be considered a horrific "mass grave," however. When done suitably, the community burial allows your pet to be buried in his or her own spot of earth without a casket. This is much like a home burial where the pet is laid to rest within the womb of Mother Earth. A community burial is not expensive and preserves your pet's memory with dignity. Your veterinarian or SPCA [Society for the Prevention of Cruelty to Animals] office can direct you regarding this type of burial arrangement.

HOW TO ARRANGE A BURIAL

For a formal burial at a pet cemetery, pre-plan the ceremony and visit several cemeteries in your area. Make a point to talk face-to-face with the cemetery's owner. Many pet cemeteries have existed for almost a century, providing excellent and proper service. Most facility owners and staff are eager to prove they are reputable and offer a dignified final resting place. Ask for references and check with local agencies or the Better Business Bureau to ensure that no complaints have been filed against the facility.

When visiting a pet cemetery, take along family members or someone close to you. The other person can offer opinions, likes and dislikes, and ask questions you hadn't thought of. The staff at the facility should be friendly and eager to offer proof of their reputation and legitimacy. They should explain every detail of how to choose a burial plot, casket, and grave marker.

Request a tour of the cemetery grounds. Look around curiously; are the grounds beautifully kept? Examine burial markers and sites; are the grave markers kept in good condition? Are weeds and grass overgrown or cut back properly? The employee who guides you on the tour should be willing to explain every detail of the cemetery. Ask any question; dumb questions are only those not asked.

Inside the facility or cemetery office, ask to see grave markers, caskets, and other items pertaining to your pet's burial. Do not allow yourself to be sold on expensive items if you find an inexpensive one that is suitable. Remember, as much as a respectable cemetery or crematory cares, their job is sales as well. Do not allow your guilt or grief to be manipulated into purchasing items you do not need or desire.

You can ask to view the freezer compartment where your pet will be on hold before burial, but don't become angered if denied. Usually the staff denies this request for your sake; viewing frozen pets upon shelves is not pleasant for anyone and the staff is concerned you will become upset. There is no real need to view this part of the facility. There is nothing hidden or negative about it. The freezer compartment guarantees the positive preservation of your pet. It is a step that must be done no matter what your feelings.

To choose a burial plot, you will tour the cemetery with an employee and choose from those available. Some plots cost more than others. A "lawn plot" may be inexpensive, compared to a plot within a grove of pine trees. If your family is present, allow your children and other members to comment on their likes and dislikes. Many times you can purchase the burial plot but wait to purchase a casket or grave marker; those items usually can be paid for and added to the contract at a later time.

Wooden caskets cost more than plastic caskets, which is another consideration. In some cases you may choose the casket lining fabric.

You can order grave markers in brass or granite and in a variety of sizes and shapes. You can also choose the inscription. The staff can write down your choices and provide an estimated total cost.

Every pet cemetery has a contract. Ask to see one in advance and read it carefully. Many contracts state that after your death, your pet's burial site can be reused. In some cases, where a payment plan is fashioned, the contract may also state that if a payment has not been made, the facility can exhume your pet's body and dispose of it in order to resell the plot. As in any business, if payments are missed, a company has the right to repossess the merchandise. That may sound terrible, but business is business. Don't let the contract terms scare you; just note every detail before proceeding. After signing the contract and making the payment, your pet's final arrangements are complete.

THE ACTUAL BURIAL

Depending on the options you choose, each burial can be unique. If your pet is deceased, the cemetery will schedule a date at the contract signing. If preplanned, at the time of death the burial date will be scheduled. Usually the pet cemetery has set aside hours when wakes, funeral proceedings, and burials take place. Some cemeteries may make exceptions to their schedule policy if absolutely necessary for your convenience. Many offer weekend burials, usually on Saturday.

On the day of your pet's burial, many preparations take place at the pet cemetery. The cemetery takes your pet out of the freezer compartment and allows him or her to resume a natural state. The staff carefully grooms your pet's body, just as at any pet grooming shop, bathes him or her, and clips their nails. The staff gives special consideration in brushing and drying your pet's fur so that it is pleasantly styled and perfumed. Rest assured that the staff is handling your pet with care and respect. Often the groomers are meticulous and careful because they are concerned that you will be pleased with your pet's appearance and that he or she will appear as you remembered.

Before you arrive, the staff gently lays your pet into his or her casket. If there is a blanket with the casket liner, the staff will often pull it up to your pet's shoulders, symbolic of peaceful rest. Your pet's head is usually laid on one side to appear as if he or she is sleeping in a beautiful, soft, and sacred bed. You may ask for your pet to be laid in another position at the time you schedule the burial, if you prefer. Some pet owners desire their pet, such as a cat, to be laid on their back with their paws in the air as if sleeping on the family couch.

The staff places the casket with your pet in a viewing room, sometimes behind folded doors that divide the casket viewing area from the rest of the room. When you arrive, the doors will be opened.

Once you arrive, an employee, usually the person you made arrangements with, greets you and helps to prepare you. Last-minute questions and concerns are discussed. He or she may then open the folding doors or open the casket for your viewing. Then the employee will exit until you are finished viewing. At this viewing time, you may conduct ritual, view your pet with family or friends, or give a loving farewell to your beloved pet.

After the viewing, the employee closes and seals the casket while you are in the room. As you witness the closing of the casket, you will know your pet is forever sealed within and will not be disturbed.

The employee will take your pet to a vehicle and drive to the burial site. You can ask to walk to the site or you may drive. Do not be afraid to ask the person who has guided you through the burial process to ride or walk with you if you prefer. He or she is present to give you sincere support and guidance and it is no imposition.

At the burial site is an opening in the earth, about six to eight feet deep, made that morning by cemetery employees. You will be able to stand at the burial site while your pet, sealed in the casket, is carefully lowered into the plot with ties or bands of sturdy nylon. Afterward, you may ask for a moment to say a prayer for your pet or perform a short ritual. Many people bring rose petals to toss on the casket as a symbol of their everlasting love and bond. When you are finished, the employees will give you the option of scattering the first bits of earth over your pet's casket, then they will begin to cover the casket with more earth. Once the site is filled, the employees use an instrument that looks like a pillar with a square base to pack the soil. They place green grass, in the shape of a cut square and appearing like a cutting of sod, on top and pack that down as well. Once done, the burial of your pet is completed. If you have chosen a grave marker, the employees will install it. If you have not chosen one yet, you can make arrangements to purchase one and have it installed later.

After the burial, you are free to remain at your pet's burial site as long as needed. You may visit anytime the cemetery is open. You will be allowed to place flowers, wreaths, religious articles, and holiday decorations at the site. Your pet is laid to rest with dignity and crosses the threshold to exist in the spiritual plane in peace.

HOME BURIAL

Informal backyard burial is a common choice for pet owners who own land or whose family or friends own land. Your decision to conduct a home burial must take into consideration the availability of land and local laws governing burial in undesignated places.

Burying your pet on your own land is extremely satisfying. You conduct every aspect of your pet's burial—complimenting your acquiring your pet in the beginning. Home burial is thought of as returning a loved animal companion to nature. There is no need for extravagance; wrapping your pet in a favorite blanket or one of your sweaters and laying him or her to rest with belongings and toys is a beautiful, loving ritual in itself.

Informal burial requires your attention to practical matters. Even if the land chosen is your property, home burial may be against the law in your area. Check with your local government offices, such as the municipal court clerk, city clerk, or police department. Find out whether or not home burial is permitted and if so whether you need to purchase a special permit. There may be certain regulations, such as the depth of the grave. The legalities exist because local officials are unable to establish control over the depth and number of informal burial plots. If a shallow grave existed, the decomposed remains could be uncovered by children or animals, causing a potential health hazard. Taking proper steps to ensure your legal rights and ability to informally bury your pet is a must. There is nothing more tragic than being told your pet needs to be moved, paying fines, attending legal proceedings, and bearing the additional heartache in your grief.

Home burial is simple, inexpensive, and satisfying, but does not guarantee a permanent, final resting place for your pet. The land may be sold in the future and used for a different purpose. A new owner may decide to build on the land or unearth your pet's grave.

If your pet dies in the winter and the ground is frozen, informal burial is impossible. Place your pet on hold with your veterinarian or local animal shelter until the ground thaws. The waiting period can be long and for some pet owners too emotionally stressful.

If home burial is your choice, call your veterinarian or a pet cemetery and ask how you may properly bury your pet. If burying your pet directly into the earth is uncomfortable, pet cemeteries and related mail-order companies offer a variety of caskets for home use.

City dwellers and individuals who rent their homes might like the option of informal burial but have no access to available land. Do not bury your pet in a public park unless the appropriate city office grants permission. Renters, even in rural areas, must also take necessary steps to acquire permission from the property owner and local government offices before burying a pet on land that is not theirs.

You may want to take a trip to the country or outstate farmlands to bury your pet in a more nature-oriented, informal area. Farmers and land owners will grant permission on occasion. Introduce yourself, explain your situation, and ask.

After home burial, you can decorate your pet's site as you wish. A friend in New Jersey placed a stone circle around her dog's burial site and planted beautiful perennial flowers, which symbolize birth, death, and rebirth. She also planted a flower garden on one side and a vegetable garden on the other. Wind chimes and decorations beautify her pet's burial site. When there is no wind, but the wind chimes still play, she says it is her dog's spirit greeting.

Unique Options

Other options exist that are costly but deserve mention. Although they may not be available at every cemetery or crematorium, contact the International Association of Pet Cemeteries listed at the end of this chapter. They can provide information about the facility closest to your area.

FREEZE-DRYING

Freeze-drying should not be confused with putting your pet on hold. Freeze-drying is a lengthy and expensive procedure where your pet is placed into any position you desire (for example, sitting or lying down) and any facial expression you desire (mouth open, mouth shut, eyes looking straight ahead). Be aware that your pet's eyes will be removed and false eyes will be put in their place. Freeze-drying preserves your pet's fur, skeleton, and appearance forever. It does so by freeze-drying internally so that only your pet's "bodily shell" remains. The cost is usually over a thousand dollars. The size of your pet, type of pet, the pet's position, and other factors affect the cost.

Specialists at the facility position your pet through an intricate holding device, much like the procedure of taxidermy. They will groom, position, and then place your pet within an enormous tank, perhaps with other pets, and switch on the freeze-drying mechanism. The process can take months to over a year to complete. Once completed, the staff removes your pet from the supporting structure and your pet is now permanently freeze-dried into position.

Many individuals place their pet in a favorite resting area in the home. At times a sanctuary is designed and the pet forever rests at home.

TAXIDERMY

This procedure is similar to freeze-drying except that your pet will be artistically prepared (such as removing and substituting the eyes) and stuffed. The process has improved over the last few years and the results are very lifelike. Taxidermy is usually less expensive than freeze-drying.

Some pet owners consult taxidermists for other preservations of their pet. Some people want to keep their pet's pelt to frame, rest on a living room furnishing, or cuddle when reminiscing. A taxidermist can provide you with many options of preserving all or a portion of your pet.

To find cemeteries or crematoriums that perform these options, look in your phone book or ask your veterinarian. If these facilities are not readily available, contact the International Association of Pet Cemeteries at the following location:

International Association of Pet Cemeteries
Executive Director
2845 Oakcrest Place
Land O' Lakes, FL 34639
800–952–5541

Make the choice for your pet's final resting place from your heart. Do not concern yourself with the opinions of insensitive others. Be pleased in knowing that your choice is for the best and expresses the undying love between yourself and your pet. The decision is an intimate one that can only be made by you with love.

Endnote

1. Sife. *The Loss of a Pet*, p. 120.

Chapter Eight

Euthanasia: A Personal Decision

ACCEPTING TOTAL RESPONSIBILITY FOR AN animal companion has its advantages and disadvantages. As human beings, we cannot control life and death, yet there are certain instances where we must make the final decision for our pet. One such case is euthanasia.

The word "euthanasia" makes animal rights advocates around the world cringe. Debates and arguments rage among animal rights supporters on this very subject. Some people see the act of euthanasia as playing god and something unnatural, while others see it as a necessary and humane relief to physical suffering, mental illness, or abused animals. The decision of euthanasia is never easy, and it is a very personal one.

I have sat lovingly, looked into my dog Sasha's eyes, and wondered about this issue. Could I bring myself to end

Sasha's suffering life if or when a terminal illness or life-threatening injury should ever happen?

During my experience in animal rescue, I witnessed animals so abused they were unfit to be trained or mentally corrected, animals so starved and parasite-infested that there was no hope for recovery. Because I had set up a home for strays and unwanted pets, I had to make decisions of whether or not to choose euthanasia. In situations where there was no medical hope, the painful choice had to be made. Luckily, these instances were rare.

Euthanasia is a legal procedure. To many pet owners, it is also a needed option. It is a part of the ultimate responsibility of pet owners who have pledged to support, protect, and make the best decision for their pet's well-being and quality of life.

Many owners question if euthanasia is the correct choice. Even those who think it is the right decision in certain situations know the choice is full of responsibility and emotional conflict. No one can ever make the decision lightly. For our own emotional well-being, we must be certain it is the only recourse to provide our pets an end to pain and suffering. We are obligated to see that our pets have comfortable, healthy, and painless lives. When the time comes to decide about euthanasia, we must feel absolutely right in the decision—for ourselves and our pets. We each have the moral and legal responsibility to decide and act accordingly. Action through love is the best way.

When pet owners consider euthanasia, emotions such as helplessness and losing control over the progress of injury or disease surface. If you choose to put off the decision, your pet may spend further days in physical agony. You may put off the decision because you want to have your pet with you. You may even inflict self-blame when you must make a decision to end your pet's life.

Euthanasia is a delicate issue, and your decision will be weighted by your personal beliefs and spiritual viewpoint. However, it is my belief that when the gods fail to act in the emergency of a suffering life, we must—in our granted ability—take the responsibility.

The next area of concern is not a spiritual consideration, but a humane one. Do we have the ethical right to take a life? Many pet owners equate an animal's life to the value of our own. Because many people believe it is not right to euthanize people, the debate is applied to animals. We have laws to sustain life support measures for our dying human loved ones, yet we are quick to end the suffering lives of other living creatures.

Many people have written living wills, a document stating what they want done in the case of a terminal illness or life-threatening injury. Many people state in their will that they do not want any form of life support given. In deciding on euthanasia for your pet, consider that he or she, in human thought-form, would want the same.

In making a final decision, however, let reality and compassion guide you. You must live with your decision so make the decision on your own. Some people will condemn your decision no matter what it is. You need to be strong. Be guided through the love of your pet and keep these four considerations in mind:

✦ From a practical viewpoint, euthanasia may be the only way to humanely eliminate the suffering and negative quality of life for your pet.

✦ Be ready to accept your decision, whether or not others agree with it.

✦ Know that you will dwell on the decision and have a sense of guilt and self-persecution—no matter what your final decision.

✦ Your spiritual beliefs about humanity's right to make a life and death decision can assist you, but it can hinder you as well.

Looking at modern viewpoints about birth may help in your decision. In our modern thought and technology, test - tube babies and artificial insemination are possible, generally accepted, and practiced, offering childless couples the great miracle of life and birth. Both types of procreation are controlled and produced by humankind. Is it wrong that out of love people seek these alternatives when natural conception is not possible? I don't think so. Why then should it be wrong to prompt death through euthanasia as a humane and loving way of ending a suffering life?

Faced with the question of whether or not to apply euthanasia, seek the advice and emotional support of a trusted friend, family, your veterinarian, or a bereavement counselor. Although you may feel this decision is too personal to share with others, the emotional support of family and friends can strengthen your efforts.

Focus upon you pet's quality of life. Is your pet suffering physical pain? Is he or she mentally ill after eating a poisonous plant or chemical, and unable to live without potentially harming himself or herself or others? After being diagnosed with cancer or other terminal illness, can your pet live comfortably and pain-free for a few more years?

When I was in junior high school, my family chose a cocker spaniel-and-poodle-mixed dog to join our family. I named her Muley. When Muley was eight years old, she developed bladder stones that required a special diet. Eventually she needed surgery. After her first surgery, she seemed back to normal, but the stones returned. We were devastated. We continued the special diet and again she required surgery. After the second surgery, she seemed to lose her zest for life. Not long after, our veterinarian told us surgery was needed again. He recommended euthanasia because he felt that Muley was not strong enough to endure surgery and that the vicious, painful cycle would continue. We were heartbroken.

My family sat down one evening to discuss Muley's quality of life. Financing the surgery was not an issue, but Muley's strength, obvious pain, and ability to survive the surgery was. A couple of days of discussion and tearful indecision went by. Ultimately, in our hearts we had already decided. Muley's quality of life was very poor; to end her suffering, euthanasia was the best choice.

Another factor that makes the decision of euthanasia difficult is that animals cannot verbally express to us how they feel. In our desire to have our pet remain, we often tell ourselves that the pet isn't suffering badly or seems healthy enough to go on. I went through this delusion with Muley. She appeared in pain, depressed, and sad in expression. I thought if we were patient and waited she would get well. There is a time when our desires must be logically evaluated. As care providers to our animal companions, we must keep in mind what is best for our pets.

Postponing the decision may seem positive for you, but is it positive for your pet? When no medical hope or cure is available, the postponement is temporary at best, and may be another way to escape the inevitable. Honor your pet's life and your love for your pet by not postponing the decision. Have the euthanasia done quickly to save your pet from additional pain and suffering and to save yourself from the emotional turmoil of delay.

Euthanasia can be the most distressing decision you will make in life—no one can pass judgment on you for choosing this necessary option. It takes the greatest love, devotion, and courage to end a suffering life. Ignore people who are critical or put them in their place. Others should respect your painful and difficult decision. At this time you need utmost support, not further emotional stress. Remove yourself from any individual who criticizes you, at least for the moment. Give yourself time to cope.

In making your decision, you should not feel you have somehow failed in the care of your pet. When no other options or hope exist, you've done great service to your pet. You have also taken tremendous strides in personal growth by knowing you made the right choice. Euthanasia can be a great act of love.

Wrongful Euthanasia

In some situations, people abuse the gift of euthanasia. Some cold-hearted, cruel individuals view euthanasia as a quick way to dispose of a pet they no longer want. Euthanasia, in this case, is a weapon of selfishness.

When an individual can no longer have a pet or does not want the pet any longer, other options exist besides euthanasia. The pet owner can look for someone to adopt the pet or can contact an animal rescue group to pick up the pet.

I am amazed that people have the energy to purposely euthanize their pet yet cannot take that same energy to call an animal rescue group to pick up the pet for future adoption.

Options and Help in the Decision

When you take your sick or injured pet to a clinic, your veterinarian will provide a diagnosis, opinion, and options. He or she will offer the truth as medically determined. Your veterinarian may tell you things you don't want to hear or that will anger you. Remember, your veterinarian has your pet's best interest at heart and there is no reason for deception.

In certain instances, your veterinarian or a friend may suggest that you seek a second opinion, which is an option. However, when your pet's quality of life deteriorates to the point when your veterinarian suggests euthanasia, he or she has usually made a correct professional decision.

How do you truly know if euthanasia is the answer? If your pet has been diagnosed with a terminal dysfunction or pain, you owe your beloved pet a dignified and painless end to suffering. Place your confidence in your veterinarian and ask for a consultation.

When making your decision, consider asking these questions:

✦ Is recovery or cure at all possible? If there is a chance, can your pet be kept on medication or somehow pain-free until further diagnosis or treatment can be done?

✦ Are the medical costs excessive and beyond your financial capabilities?

✦ Will keeping your pet alive—knowing he or she is suffering—or enduring the wait for further treatment give you excessive emotional strain and suffering as well?

If your pet is a part of your family, let everyone—including children—know that a decision needs to be made. If you have made the decision, gently speak with your child and ask for input. There should be no arguing; use only soothing explanations and persuasion. (See Chapter 3 for more information on bereavement and children.)

The Euthanasia Procedure

When you choose euthanasia for your pet, the veterinarian prepares a syringe containing a massive overdose of a barbiturate or sedative. Some veterinarians use two different injections. Once the injection is given, your pet no longer feels pain and suffering and gently but swiftly slips into sleep and peaceful death. Although euthanasia is not painful for the pet, it is often painful for the witnessing pet owner. As the veterinarian gives the injection, you may see a beautiful expression of peace and painlessness in your pet's eyes—almost an expression of utopia. Shortly afterward, the pet achieves a peaceful death.

During the procedure, many pet owners hold and cuddle their beloved pet, watch the pain and suffering disappear, and bid a loving farewell. I feel that if you are strong enough to be there, you should be there. Think how much more comfortable your pet will feel in your presence. You are your pet's entire life—his or her partner in unconditional love. Your presence will exemplify the love you have for your pet. Though this is not the final moment of your relationship—your bond will transform to a spiritual one—your presence is the final gesture of love on the physical plane.

Witnessing euthanasia prompts different emotions in individuals—many of these emotions can be overwhelming. You may experience sadness in not wanting to let go of the physical bond with your pet. You may feel tremendous happiness in knowing your pet is now released from physical pain. Many individuals claim that the experience was a spiritual and loving episode. Others say that the experience was very sad, yet there was a feeling of completion and knowledge that they had made the right, humane choice.

There is nothing wrong with being unable to be present during the procedure. Do not feel you must or should be present. It hurts immensely to cuddle your pet, knowing he or she will no longer be with you in this world. As spiritualists, we realize the Gods and Goddesses have given us blessings and the power to act as we deem best for all of nature. Granted the divine power of reasoning and the ability to save another living creature from agony, know in your heart that your action shows ultimate love and mercy. Do not allow yourself the torturous feelings of guilt or blame.

Know that most veterinarians are emotionally upset by this procedure as well, even though they administer euthanasia during their work. Some veterinarians will stay with you after the injection to provide support, while others leave the room, providing privacy. Both actions are gestures of caring and done in your best interest. Let your veterinarian know beforehand what you would like them to do. This will help you and your veterinarian during this emotionally difficult procedure.

Some veterinarians do not allow pet owners to witness euthanasia, due to unpleasant experiences the veterinarian has had during his or her practice. It is not unusual for pet owners to become emotionally distraught and respond negatively. An individual may faint or possibly hurt themselves from tumultuous emotions. If your veterinarian does not permit witnessing, know that he or she is not hiding anything. If you are not comfortable with that policy, however, consider euthanasia with another veterinarian who allows witnessing.

In choosing euthanasia, we touch the other side—the darkness of death—and learn more about our inner selves. This option is never a simple choice. You must fight back the guilt, blame, and self-defeat and look at yourself as a courageous, compassionate individual. You have shared time in your life with your dear pet where you were strengthened as an individual.

Your pet has transformed your life and made you a better person through the beautiful, loving experience of being its guardian and companion. You've adored your pet in life, and through spiritual connection you will both continue to adore and love each other.

Chapter Nine

Other Forms
of Pet Loss

PET LOSS EXTENDS BEYOND THE SEPARATION
inevitable through physical death. There are instances in
life—some which are unavoidable—when you lose your
pet because you must give him or her away due to a change
in your living situation, or he or she runs away. These situations cause grief similar to that experienced in a physical death.

The difference between bereavement due to physical
separation and bereavement due to physical death is that in
separation you know your pet continues to live on without
you, many times with another individual. This type of grief
includes anxiety about your pet's happiness and safety in a
new environment, and acceptance of your pet's new life.

Pet lovers are devastated when a situation arises where
they must give away a beloved pet. Many pet owners consider their pets as surrogate children; the owners examine

and try every available option. Sadly, there are occasions when options are nonexistent.

Giving Up Your Pet

As much as each and every pet lover dreads it, situations exist when a pet can no longer remain in a family. Unexpected instances arrive where our devotion and love for a pet cannot overcome the obstacle of needed or forced change in our lives. While many possible options may exist, when they are attempted and fail, it is time for a serious change. Below are several situations that pose a risk to pet ownership and some viable options.

Allergic Reaction

If someone in your family develops an allergic reaction to your pet's dander, speak with your family physician or an allergist at once. An allergic reaction can be serious and result in respiratory problems and related symptoms. An allergist can assess the matter and provide a course of action. Ask the doctor about medication to control the reaction. Confine your pet to a certain area of your home to decrease the dander.

Other suggestions for reducing the dander include reducing the amount of fabric in your home, ridding your home of carpeting, using blinds instead of curtains, and housing your pet outside. Housing your pet outdoors, or confining your pet to one area of your home are good choices if your pet's quality of life is not adversely affected.

When viable options and allergy shots fail, the only solution may be to find your pet a new home. This can be emotionally overwhelming to you and the family member who developed the reaction, especially if that member is a child. Frequently, a child will resent his or her own body, feeling betrayed by it. In making any decision, your child's quality of life—and that of your pet—must be carefully considered.

RELOCATION

A job transfer and move to a new residence where pets are not allowed has limited options. You could remain in the employment and residence already held, but sacrificing the new employment may not be an option. Your only option might be to search for another job.

If the new employer is paying for your family move and has chosen the new residence, which is a common practice in corporations, request a move to a residence allowing pets.

You need to assess whether the new job transfer is an important step for you and your family and the options available to you regarding your pet. If all other options fail, your pet will need a new home.

TENANTS

Individuals who rent find themselves dealing with a limited number of landlords willing to allow pets. If at all possible, try to remain in the current rental dwelling and search for another landlord who allows pets. Place a personal ad in the newspaper to search for rental property allowing pets.

Moving to a suitable residence and keeping your pet are the best options, though sometimes that is easier said than done. If buying a house or mobile home is impossible, or if an immediate move is necessary, you have limited choices.

Tenants who do not have a signed lease between themselves and a landlord can find themselves issued with eviction or court notice for having a pet. There may in fact have been a verbal agreement, but unless the landlord specifies in writing that pets are allowed on the premises, tenants are at risk. If a tenant cannot solve the issue with the landlord and keep the pet, loses a court case, or cannot afford the cost of a lawsuit, there are only two options: attempt to relocate or place the pet for adoption.

A New Marriage

If you are a pet owner in a new marriage and find that your loving spouse is unable to tolerate your pet, try to uncover the reasons and find a positive solution. The reason may be a phobia or a general dislike. Keep your pet outdoors or confine the pet to a certain area of your living space (but determine if your pet will have a positive quality of life with the new option).

This situation can become stressful as you must weigh the new marriage against the love for the pet. It is not uncommon for the marriage to be preserved and the pet placed for adoption.

A New Baby

First-time parents who have a pet may find that once their newborn baby is brought home, the pet poses risks to the child. Frequently, the pet in this situation is a large dog.

Keep in mind, however, that pets rarely pose a risk to children—the exception are untrained pets or ones with a history of destructive tendencies. Options include taking your pet to obedience classes, discussing the situation with your veterinarian, or creating a schedule where your pet and new baby do not come in contact with each other until your child is older, such as allowing your pet the run of the house only when your child sleeps.

Hours of Employment

A job promotion, new work hours, or required travel may create a problem in your pet's care and quality of life. If you cannot find someone to help care for your pet while you are working or traveling, consider your pet's quality of life. Consider searching for new employment, hiring a pet sitter, or if no other options are possible, placing your pet for adoption.

Financial Problems

In our modern human lives, corporate downsizing, unemployment, and financial hardship are a reality. Financial instability causes risk to pet ownership. The cost of food, medical care, and other pet-related necessities can be a problem.

If you experience financial hardship and are unable to take advantage of the options listed in this chapter, finding your pet a new home, for the well-being of your family and your pet, may be a necessity.

The Elderly

The financial restraints and health problems of the elderly pose a risk to their pet ownership. Frequently, older individuals move to senior-citizen apartment complexes that do not allow pets. If you are in this situation, ask your family members or someone else you trust to help you search for options. If your separation from your beloved pet is inevitable, however, enjoy the remaining time with your pet.

If the final outcome is to find your pet a new home, realize that your love for your pet is not in question. You might think that everyone will condemn you for making the necessary decision of giving away your cherished and precious companion. Recognize this feeling and assumption as guilt, a cruel symptom of your grief. Do not emotionally batter yourself.

How to Cope

After your family has come to terms with the matter, enjoy the remaining time with your pet. Your child may spend every free moment with the pet, which is fine and should not be discouraged.

Separation from your pet when circumstances demand it causes guilt, disbelief at the reality, and initial unacceptance. Allow everyone to speak freely about the upcoming separation.

Guilt is an emotion we inflict upon ourselves relentlessly and wrongfully. When you have done all you can and tried your best to seek options, allow your mind peace from self-reprimand. Take that negative energy and concentrate on acquiring a safe, secure, and happy new home for your pet. You know you are a good caretaker and can sometimes overcome the odds, but if you cannot change the reality, you must cope.

Your pet can sense your feelings and emotions. He or she knows when something is wrong with you or when you are deeply upset. When they surface, these painful and negative emotions can stress your pet. Try to enjoy your remaining time together and project positive energies to make the situation comfortable for both of you. Later, as you reflect, you will have the peace of mind that your last days together were happy ones.

Hidden in your deep love for your pet is the idea that only you can best provide for him or her. We pride ourselves on being animal lovers and providers. It is unwise, however, to assume that no other human being can provide as we do.

Some people who must give up their pet choose to have their healthy pet euthanized. Usually, these people assume that no one else can provide the proper care and love, but this is a selfish thought. Euthanasia, however, is usually only an option when a pet is unhealthy or otherwise incapable of functioning around other people. If you are in this situation, take time to reconsider pet adoption. Consider the numerous good homes and loving families wanting a pet like yours to love, care for, and cherish. There is no reason to rob your pet of the opportunity to experience love and happiness in a new environment. Your worries of whether or not your pet can cope with the change and continue a happy life are typical, as are concerns that his or her new life be free from abuse and neglect.

Using an Organization to Find a Good Home

When you have decided to find a new home for your pet, ask all your family members to write down their concerns about the potential new environment and life for your pet. Voicing concerns and desires makes a difference and can ease the process.

If searching for a new home yourself is too painful, contact a local pet rescue or adoption organization through your telephone book, your veterinarian, local pound, or state kennel club (choose one that does not apply euthanasia to those pets not adopted in a specific period of time). A pet adoption organization can ease the stress and emotional pain of looking for a new home. Non-profit organizations with foster homes are the best choice. As you look for an organization, call each one, present your questions and concerns, and continue searching until you find a group that is satisfactory. Ask a member of the group to visit your home and meet with you and your pet. This will provide an opportunity for you to analyze the individual, learn of the group's activities, and comfort your worries.

Once you've chosen an organization, know that the staff will take the utmost care in interviewing potential new owners and providing a comfortable environment for your pet in the process. Foster homes are loving families who provide care and a stable home environment. Many times, foster home families adopt the pet in their care.

INTERVIEWING POTENTIAL HOMES

In interviewing potential new owners yourself, you have complete control of where your pet will start a new life. You will, however, need to schedule interviews and welcome strangers into your home. If you live alone, have a friend or relative with you when people arrive.

To find potential owners, place an ad in a local paper. Personal ads do not cost much and, out of all the responses, there is a good chance that many will be suitable homes. Another option is to ask your veterinarian if he or she can recommend a new home or tell other clients that your pet is available for adoption. Another client of your veterinarian is an ideal owner. Visiting the veterinarian regularly demonstrates the individual is a good care provider.

Before the interview, prepare your list of concerns as well as a list of questions. Below are some suggestions (you can ask some of these questions during an initial telephone interview).

Does the potential owner have other pets? If so, ask him or her to bring the pet to your home to interact with yours. I remember a couple who came to our home in response to an ad for a foster dog we had, a Rottweiler named Duke. I suggested they bring their eight-year-old dog with them, which they did. The two dogs did not get along. The meeting saved the dogs, us, and them from the possible trouble that could have occurred had they adopted Duke.

Does the potential owner have children? If so, ask him or her to bring the children. If the children dislike your pet or mistreat your pet, you will be present to witness it. From the children's reaction and behavior, you can decide if the home is suitable.

Does the potential owner rent housing? If the person rents, ask for a signed notice from the landlord stating that your pet will be allowed to live on the premises. From my experience in the pet adoption league, some people who rent may adopt your pet only to have the landlord tell them to get rid of the pet. The new owners may take the pet to a pound, put it out on the street, or give it away.

What outdoor activities will your pet, especially a dog, have with the new owner? Ask also if the property has a fenced-in yard, a kennel, or a tie-out leash. Find out if the property is near a busy highway.

What hours do the parents work? This is an important question to ask when interviewing a family. Never accept the answer that a child will care for the pet. Although children may want a pet, the actual care for the pet is usually the parents' responsibility. If both parents work ten-hour days and are rarely home, take that fact into consideration.

These questions are typical of ones asked by adoption service groups. Such groups are very strict in interviewing and reject more homes than they accept. Use the same caution when you interview prospective owners. Do not feel uncomfortable with interrogating people. People who sincerely wish to adopt your pet will be open and understanding of your concerns. Reject anyone who refuses to answer or provide essential proof, like landlord permission.

During an interview, if you sense the prospective owner is unsuitable, thank them for their interest and state that you are considering another family. You can add that if the family decides against the adoption, you will notify them. Any rejection should be polite.

Once you have chosen a home, record the new family's physical address, not mailing address, and a telephone number. After a couple of days, drive to the new owner's home. If it appears the people have lied (for example, they live in an apartment complex instead of a private home) or if anything looks undesirable or suspicious, stop and confront the new owner. Do not jump to conclusions, however; there may be a misunderstanding. Discuss the problem with the owners on a positive note and negotiate a solution.

SAYING GOOD-BYE

When the moment arrives to say good-bye to your pet, there will be tears and deep sorrow. Be certain to begin saying farewell before the new owner or the pet adoption volunteer arrives. When other people are present, we as humans tend to clam up and don't express ourselves the way we would like to. Remember, whoever comes to your home for your pet realizes the agony you feel. Taking away a precious part of someone's life is painful in itself.

When the new owner is present, try not to prolong the farewell more than necessary. It is common for the new owner and the grieving owner to both show sadness. While this is fine, you do not want to stress your pet or the new owner. They both have much excitement and change to deal with in becoming acquainted.

Runaway and Stolen Pets

During my involvement with the pet adoption league, my husband and I fostered an eleven-year-old schnauzer. A local pound had picked up the dog in an urban area. Later, a group volunteer for the adoption league had taken him from the pound. The league brought the dog to us and he became one of the family. Because of his age, temperament, and nature, I was certain he was lost and from a good home.

After two weeks, the adoption league called. They had placed an ad for the dog in the urban area's local newspaper and had received a response. The dog's family lived miles away from where the dog had been found—he must have wandered aimlessly trying to get home. When the owners arrived at our home, the little gray schnauzer leapt upon them in glee. The three reunited in tears and great joy and excited barks. I stood by, tearful, witnessing a reunion that could have easily never happened.

The owners told me that their dog had become lost on Thanksgiving Day, when the family had relatives over for dinner. With all the visitors, the front door was opened more frequently and longer than usual. The schnauzer was never allowed outdoors alone, but that day he decided to stroll out the door, unnoticed in the swarm of visiting relatives.

Numerous situations like the one above can suddenly occur, resulting in a runaway pet. A dog's outdoor leash breaks or the dog escapes from an outdoor kennel. A cat waltzes out a door accidentally left open or escapes through a broken window screen. The sudden instinct to chase another animal may lead a pet astray. Birds sometimes escape from their cages and leave through an open window or door.

When a pet runs away, many owners ask themselves why such a terrible incident has happened. Accidental mishaps can overcome even the greatest of care and control over a pet. When that happens, owners can easily turn their anger, disbelief, and regret inward to punish themselves.

The joy of finding and reclaiming a lost pet is a reunion desperately sought but rarely possible. Even though you may have made every effort to find your pet, you may need to realize and accept the loss.

Stolen pets are definitely beyond our control. A thief is a calculating individual who stalks victims without their knowledge. Usually the perpetrator analyzes the environment and acts only when he or she is certain no witnesses are present.

People steal pets for many reasons. Some perpetrators steal a pedigreed pet because they want to own that breed and cannot afford to purchase one themselves. Some people steal pets and sell them to laboratories that test products on animals or conduct scientific testing (many laboratories, however, are changing their policies and stopping their animal testing). There are also cases where an individual steals a pet merely to collect the reward money from the desperate owner.

You are not to blame if your pet is stolen. No matter what protective and careful measures you take daily, or would have taken, the intruder wanted your pet and would have found a way to steal him or her. When your pet is gone, it seems inconceivable that another human being would dare destroy the loving relationship between you and your pet.

Once you realize your pet has run away or been stolen, grief surfaces. You know that your pet is still living and you worry for his or her well-being. There exists immediate desperation to find your pet and save him or her from possible harm. You need to face the fact that other individuals may be caring for or harming your pet. These thoughts, coupled with bereavement, are nearly unbearable, but there is action you can take to begin the search for your pet. Have faith.

What to Do

Your pet has run away or been stolen and the situation seems unreal. Amid the shock, disbelief, denial, and anger, you are in a panic. Take time to come to terms with the situation and then plan how to explain the loss to your family, especially your children. Telling others is difficult because in your own shock and sorrow, you may barely be capable of understanding the circumstances and what should be done.

Gather your family into a comfortable room and inform them of the situation. Be open and honest. When questions arise of how, when, and why the situation happened, state the details and answer truthfully. Assure your children that although you do not have all the answers, with their help the family will try its best to get answers and find the pet.

Below is a list of actions that will help you to recover your pet and obtain answers.

✦ Place a personal ad in your local newspaper's classified ad section right away. The cost is minimal and may reach someone who has at least seen your pet. Many times, someone has seen an animal wandering or walking down a neighborhood street. In thinking that the animal is a neighbor's pet, they will not stop and take the animal home. Finding out what area your pet has recently been in will help to track your pet.

✦ Create signs that are easily read from a distance. Use fluorescent construction paper with information written in bold markers to capture people's attention. On the sign, include your pet's breed, name, age, color of eyes, fur pattern and color(s), and your address and telephone number.

Place the signs on telephone poles in your neighborhood. Ask if you can hang your sign in local businesses such as laundromats, grocery stores, libraries, schools, parking lots, restaurants, and other public places frequented by people day and night.

If you offer a reward for information or the return of your pet, do not list the amount of money on your sign. If the reward is attractive, you could receive a number of false calls. Beware of anyone who asks you to forward money by mail, bank transfer, or other means in exchange for the safe return of your pet. Unless the person arrives at your home with your pet, do not provide reward money.

When my mother's cat ran away, she designed large, eye-catching signs complete with an actual photo of her cat. She placed them at her local deli, department stores, and grocery stores. A couple of weeks later, an individual telephoned her to say that he had seen her cat killed on a local highway. The individual had seen my mother's sign in a department store. If she had not posted her signs, she would have never known what had happened.

✦ If you believe your pet was stolen, call the police and file a report. If your pet is found, the police report will enable you to prosecute the thief and possibly save other pet owners from suffering the same loss. The police may already have a record of cases in your area and your notifying them could help your search as well as that of other pet owners. The police will also advise you of local pounds, animal shelters, and other establishments to contact to find out if your pet is being held there.

✦ Contact animal shelters and pounds within a twenty-mile radius around your town; lost pets can wander and cover a great distance. Also contact veterinarians, animal control officials, forest rangers in state parks, business owners, neighbors, all pet-related businesses, and rescue or adoption organizations. Each business you contact will provide you with more places to look. Your search will be perpetuated with each contact.

✦ Visit local pounds and animal shelters and leave a photo of your pet with them. If volunteers or employees work different shifts, everyone will be able to refer to the photo when new animals arrive.

COPING WITH THE LOSS

Know that your pet did not purposely run away from you. When pets run away, they are usually following their instinct to chase another animal, wander the land, and follow curious scents of other living creatures. Pets do not run away from loving homes because they no longer love them. The exchange of love and devotion between pet owner and pet is far too great.

Your pet will always love you. There is no question of this. Accept the fact that something caught your pet's attention and triggered an instinct that caused his or her sudden departure.

Replacing a runaway or stolen pet for the sake of your children or yourself can be a positive action. Remember, however, to give the entire family time to grieve. For the health of body, mind, and spirit, allow the emotions of grief to surface.

If your runaway or stolen pet is not returned, know in your heart that you have done the best you could. Constant worrying of your pet's well-being will shadow you, but it is important to consider that another loving owner may have found your pet. After attempting to search for your pet, there is nothing more you can do but hope for your pet's safety and happiness.

Using Ritual to Cope with Loss

In order to endure the emotional roller coaster of loss and begin the search for your loved one, you must maintain inner energy and strength. Gathering every ounce of strength within, when the reality around you seems to be deteriorating, is not an easy task. The feeling of loss is not only focused on the physical loss of your pet but the unpleasant sense that a loss of control has ensued in your life. Faith is challenged as we struggle with the understanding of "why" through disbelief and utter dismay.

Practitioners of pagan spiritualism realize that grief is a result of the mysterious cycles of life and nature. Each cycle has a beginning, end, and new beginning. This is true of pet bereavement caused by runaway or stolen pets. There may be mystery as to why the situation came into existence, but we know that no matter the reason, the pet will continue living. You need to focus on this truth. Your pet has not disappeared from the web of life. There is always hope for a reunion upon the physical plane and beyond. Communion with your pet is not merely a physical one. Your bond and love with your pet exceeds time and space. Similar to loss of a pet through physical death, you need to accept that your relationship with your pet has gone through a cycle of transition.

Now is a time when you need spiritual faith and strength. You will journey within and outside of yourself for a sense of understanding. It may seem these factors are greatly hindered by seemingly unanswered inquiries asked of your God or Goddess. You may wonder why the precious love of your pet has been taken away. It doesn't seem fair.

Ritual allows for soul searching and exploring the unknown in search of answers. Through ritual, we gain a clearer understanding of life and a rejuvenation of self. We begin building the foundation to regain control of our lives through magic, spiritualism, and strengthening of self.

Self-exploratory rites to understand and touch the core of inner resources can benefit you most at this trying time. Rites of healing—ones that heal the self—can render resolution to overcome the grief and continue healthy living (see the Ritual of Psychic Connection outlined below). These types of rituals can double the effect of inner healing and reclaim emotional strength.

Your first and foremost concern before healing and self-exploration is psychic communion with your pet. Separation from your pet, whether through physical death or separation in life, causes feelings of love lost. It is natural to want to rekindle the contact with your pet. Through our desperation to find a lost pet or restore health and vitality to a terminally ill pet, we often become obsessive and illogical because we fear the loss of such a pure, innocent, loving bond. Realize that physical separation does not mean a divorce of your loving bond.

In our hearts we know that love forever bonds us to loved ones, whether or not they are with us. Your memories, your pet's memories, and the power of love grants eternal nexus. Depending upon your personal and spiritual beliefs, it can be said that as long as you have the memories and love, your pet is forever with you in spiritual union. The longing you have to experience the bond can be made possible by psychic connecting.

Psychic and ritual work spiritually connect you with your pet. Communion through the medium of love and the life force in all creatures makes this possible.

Conducting such a ritual, however, may not result in your pet's return home if he or she is missing. Perhaps the most important principle is experiencing the loving bond that will exist between you and your pet even through this separation. In doing so, you will come to accept the loss and work toward resolution.

RITUAL OF PET PSYCHIC CONNECTION

The purpose of this ritual is to prompt healing within you and make psychic contact with your lost or stolen pet. The ritual can project energies of protection to your lost pet and assist you in regaining a sense of control in your traumatic situation, revitalizing your faith, and maintaining a connection with your pet.

You may conduct this ritual ceremonially or casually. Casting a magical circle or following preparation procedures of your spiritual practice is ideal to connect with your deity, empower your faith, and reclaim inner strength. Alter and enhance the ritual by your own practices. This version is based upon contemporary pagan Shamanic practices, suitable for most practitioners, regardless of spiritual or magical belief systems.

What You'll Need: Dried mugwort (*artemesia vulgaris*; you can purchase the fresh leaves of this herb at some health food shops, through herb mail-order catalogs, and in New

Age shops); a rattle or drum; your choice of incense, candles, and other ritual tools and decoration; personal belongings of your pet.

Preparations: Schedule your ritual when privacy is available. It can be conducted indoors or outdoors. Avoid being
interrupted by the phone or television and individuals,
other than those who may work with you in the ritual.

If you conduct this ritual outdoors, you may choose to
wear street clothes if privacy is uncertain. Performing the
rite wearing your ritual robe is ideal. Practitioners often
choose robes and tabards with the idea that wearing ritual
clothing allows for a mystical atmosphere and assists in
shifting awareness to obtain ritual consciousness. The color
of the ritual garments or street clothes can lend magical
properties as well. Skyclad can be chosen with the belief
that a clothed body cannot emit personal energies and
power effectively. Ultimately, the decision is yours.

Set up your altar with ritual tools you want to incorporate into this ritual, the mugwort, incense to burn for purification, rattle or drum, candles, and your pet's personal
belongings to aid in acquiring psychic connection.

1. Conduct your circle casting or other opening exercise,
   such as purification of your sacred space, as you normally would in your spiritual practice. After doing so, sit in
   the center of your sacred space. Meditate for a moment
   on the purpose of your ritual and what you hope to gain
   from it. Concentrate on your pet's safe return home and
   focus on your state of being to evolve strength, faith,
   and the ability to emotionally cope.

Place the rattle or drum and mugwort leaves on the floor or ground in the center of your sacred space.

2. Hold the rattle or drum and stand in the center of your sacred space, facing north. (North is the sacred direction where the sun passes at night and represents the depths of the unconscious mind. This direction is ideal for your psychic work. In Wicca, the north is considered the home of the deities and the traditional, most sacred direction of the elements.) Pivot sunwise once, shaking your rattle or beating your drum while visualizing the creation of an inner circle around your being. This is to cleanse and purify yourself and your sacred space, as well as construct a shield against negative or obstructing energy in preparation for your psychic work.

3. Return to facing north. Shake your rattle or beat your drum downward from your chest toward the floor to invoke the northern element of Earth and open the passage into the lower world of Mother Earth. Speak words of power, such as:

I invoke thee, O element of the North. By the gift of earthly power given to me of Mother Earth, I open the passage of the lower world of nature. By this, the first channel is opened.

Visualize white streams of energy entering the soles of your feet and flowing up your entire being. Feel their warmth, vibration, and energy.

4. Stand in the center of your sacred space. Play your instrument at your chest to open the passage into your inner self and speak sacred words, such as:

Empowered by my ancestors and the divine wisdom of the Old Ones, I gather strength within me and break the ties that bind me consciously to this material world. By this, the second channel, the passage to my higher self, is opened.

Feel yourself open within. Your own energies are swirling in the streams of white light from Mother Earth. Your chest may physically feel lighter with a tickling sensation.

5. Stand in the center of your circle and raise your instrument to the heavens. Open the passage to the upper, spiritual world, and speak sacred words, such as:

   Through the divine power granted to me by God [or Goddess], I open the sacred passage to the spirit world. Hence, the sacred trinity of channels has been opened. I stand in the center of Universal Oneness and the Web of Life—succeeding space and time for my psychic work.

   Visualize golden light streaming quickly from above you and entering into the crown of your head. Feel the warm, pulsating energy course through your entire being.

6. Sit down. White and gold swirls of combined earth and celestial energy circle you. Continue to rattle or drum in a rhythmic beat. Listen to the entrancing beat of your instrument. The rhythmic sound is symbolic of the divine heartbeat of all existence. Feel your own energy weaving into the earth and celestial energies. Clear your mind for a moment and feel your mind unfold from the physical restraints of this world.

7. Stop playing your instrument and gently set it down beside you. Take the dried mugwort leaves into hand. Sit comfortably in the center of your sacred space. Between your thumb and index finger, crush the leaves and state:

By Mother Earth's gift of mugwort,
the shadowy world of the seer opens to me.
Sacred herb of the ancient seers,
Like my ancestors, I bathe in your essence.
I cross oceans of time—guide me through the
  sacred, psychic channels.

(Crushing the mugwort between your thumb and index finger relaxes your conscious mind and awakens your deep consciousness.)

8. Rub the leaves together in front of your nose—not directly beneath it. Gently inhale. Do not snort the mugwort. (Inhaling the odor of the fresh, crushed leaves with visualization promotes psychic awareness.[1] Please note, however, that the essential oil of mugwort is hazardous and is not recommended for use.)

Visualize the secular world around you melting away, and a peaceful, celestial environment of unlimited darkness and stars surrounding you, swallowing you. This is the realm of Universal Oneness. Allow yourself to be totally absorbed. You feel that everything is a part of you, and you are a part of everything in existence.

9. Sprinkle the mugwort to the ground or floor around you. Calm your conscious mind of daily worries and mundane concerns. Relax your body and mind. Continue to visualize the vast darkness of space and glittering

stars, and the white and gold streams of universal energy circling your being.

Sit with your spine straight, and your head up to align your neck's cervical spine. Lower your shoulders. Allow your muscles to relax. Rest your weary mind. Visualize and feel the heavens surrounding you.

When your mind has unfolded and unconscious levels ascended, you may feel a sense of projecting out of your physical body. This is to be expected.

10. Stop visualizing. Clear your mind completely. Only peace and clarity surround you. Rest for a moment.

Visualize a mist that develops then slowly dissipates. You find yourself in the midst of an extravagant garden. Visualize the sacred garden. You are seated upon moist, fertile, rich soil. Surrounding you is a labyrinth of green shrubbery and endless flowers of exquisite, unworldly beauty. The flowers around you are of unique composition and vibrant, individual colors. Before you is a separate bed of nine flowers, arranged in three rows and three columns. You are within the Garden of the Goddess, which offers healing and wisdom.

Each flower is a different species, with individual properties to assist you in the healing and psychic connection with your pet. Visualize them arranged in three rows:

Flower	Attribute
First row	
Red Rose	Love, strength, vitality
Gold Lily	Acceptance of transformation in life
Black Iris	Absorption of fear

Flower	Attribute
Second row	
Purple Pansy	Guidance toward resolution
Blue Viola	Calm of emotions, perception
Green Ivy	Intuition, inner healing
Third row	
White Mum	Peace, revitalization of higher self
Yellow Gladiolus	Protection of a loved one
Orange Marigold	Adaptability of transformation

Gazing upon the beauty of the flower bed, pick each flower whose qualities are needed for your balance and healing. The flowers project positive qualities for your absorption so that you may prepare for the psychic communion with your pet. You can only be of strength or guidance to your pet after first conjuring such in yourself.

Visualize streaming colors of the energy each flower emits, absorbing them into your being. You breathe deeply the sweet, refreshing floral aroma of the Goddess' garden. The color rays are warm, protective, and revitalizing to your soul.

Sit with your gathered flowers. Concentrate on each and on the qualities each provides you. Allow yourself to begin internal healing.

Know that you and your pet are eternally bound in spirit, in psychic mind, and in the divine realm of your deity. Know that although your physical life together has been abruptly ended, nothing can destroy the love you and your pet have forever.

Meditate on positive thoughts. Find acceptance within yourself. Note the transformation from the physical bond of love with your pet to a spiritual, psychic bond. There has been no end, but a new beginning in which you both will adapt and continue to love.

11. Lay your chosen flowers on the rich, dark soil next to you. Their amplified energies have made you feel strong and rejuvenated in mind and body. You are ready to make the psychic connection with your pet.

Visualize the fertile, brown soil of the garden before you caving inward at the flower roots. The flowers disappear in the shifting, sinking soil. An enormous hole is revealed in the earth; a tunnel of twisting roots, earthworms, and quartz crystals forms. The tunnel represents your separation but also the undying love and connection you and your pet have against all odds.

Rise to your knees and lower yourself into the dark earth. Having projected from your physical shell, it is no struggle for you to travel the winding, rough soil tunnel. Once you reach the other end of the tunnel, you are united with your pet's aura. Now is the time to amplify messages, strength, positive energies, and love to your pet. Take as much time as you need.

Allow your feelings to surface. Communicate to your pet the loss you feel and your love. Do not allow your desires to make unrealistic promises you may not be able to complete. Promising success may lead to guilt and regret later if you are unable to find your pet. State that you will do everything in your power to locate and reunite with your pet; this is a legitimate promise.

When you have completed your communication with your pet, send a final message that the communication is near an end. You can always renew yourself at the Goddess' Garden or visit your pet through the tunnel again in the future.

12. In closing the ritual, you may simply end with a moment of meditation and reflection. You may wish to write your experience in a journal. Thereafter, close your sacred space.

Many contemporary pagans who have practiced this ritual claim to reunite with their pet in a "light body." Some individuals visualized themselves and their pet as separate auras of flowing energy. Others state that ghostly spirit doubles of their physical bodies reunited at the tunnel's end. How you envision your reunion with your pet is a unique, intimate experience. You may sense your pet's presence or visualize him or her.

Do not be concerned that psychic communication or the reunion through the tunnel may confuse or upset your pet should he or she be in another person's care or adjusting to a new environment. In my opinion, any positive, unselfish energies and psychic transmittal you provide can only benefit your pet. You may receive messages from your pet that will ease your mind in knowing he or she is happy and well, and that is another benefit.

Ritual will help you to heal and strengthen yourself, and you are then able to celebrate the loving bond forever between you and your pet.

Ritual is meant to be a positive action toward understanding, acceptance, and healing. If you continue to dwell upon the negative factors in your pet's disappearance, which may or may not be reality, you will prolong your grief and miss praising the love between you. Rejoice in the memories, hope for the best, and celebrate your eternal love.

Endnote

1. Cunningham. *Magical Aromatherapy*, p. 114.

Chapter 10

Pet Bereavement & Spirituality

THROUGHOUT THIS TEXT, THE CONTEMPORARY pagan spiritual viewpoint regarding death has been explored. This chapter elaborates on the pagan spiritual view but also investigates how other spiritual belief systems view pet death.

You cannot discuss the subject of death without referring to spiritual beliefs. Through religion, we hope to unite with deity or become divine in order to be granted an afterlife. All religions of the world have sacred teachings regarding death; death is the magnet that pulls us closer to deity through spiritualism.

Throughout history, our ancestors have sought understanding and preparation of death from the province of religion. Ages ago, the wise man/woman, medicine man/woman, clergy, and appointed priesthoods of all civilizations were the only acknowledged authorities on the

subject. The exceptions included the metaphysical philosophers, soothsayers, and individuals deemed as practicing
occult sciences.

Today our lifestyles, attitudes, and ideas about death
have changed. Many individuals have beliefs about death
and the afterlife that were not taught through a traditional
family religion. Science has allowed us to gain new theories
of human existence that affect our viewpoint of death as
well. The rapid growth of contemporary pagan religion and
religious practice of the ancients has revitalized some archa-
ic considerations of death. No longer is "hellfire and brim-
stone" considered the destiny of humanity. The powerful
propaganda of death has been used as a weapon or a manip-
ulative tool to drive fear into those unwilling to conform to
certain religious standards. Today these scare tactics have
been discarded for the most part as individuals strive for
their own sense of spiritualism and divinity.

The keeping of pets for pleasure and companionship
had originally been the practice of nobility and landed gen-
try.[1] Throughout humanity's history we find evidence of animals earning a place as pets by displaying helpful behavior
to humanity (such as the cat's role in saving Europe from
the plague). Civilizations such as the ancient Egyptians and
Sumerians found positive qualities of animals in their obser-
vance. These positive attributes earned many animals a role
in religious and magical practices (for example, in Egypt cats
were regarded as sacred).

Gradually, as leisure and wealth spread, keeping pets for
human pleasure became popular. The satisfaction of owning
a personal pet attracted many people. As the human population grew, so did the pet population.

With the evolving interest in pet ownership, public awareness about animal rights and various pet issues came into being. This created initial understanding of the human-pet bond. In turn, the increased awareness and love of animals as pets caused many grieving pet owners to ask what happens to their beloved pets at death. Questions were raised as to whether or not animals had souls, if they would find sanctuary in the realm of the Gods, and if pet owners would be reunited with their pets in the afterlife. Historically, these questions were scoffed at and ignored.

Modern-day religious and magical practitioners who have animal companions have introduced the question of what organized religion can do to help the bereaved pet owner. In some cases, when a pet owner asks spiritual clergy for compassion and counsel, they are told that help is not available. The bereaved pet owner may in fact divorce his or her religion all together when he or she finds that there seems to be no love, concern, or spiritually uplifting perspective.

Every religion contains considerations of birth, life, and death, and a form of rebirth. Most provide some insight into the human-animal bond. Simply because a religious doctrine does not discuss pet care or pet death does not make it unsuitable for your needs at this time. Every spiritual belief system offers some form of enlightenment.

Perhaps the best enlightenment can be found within yourself. Armed with your spiritual faith and practices, look within to find truth. Ritual, meditation, and positive thought will prompt your healing. You will be granted divine answers and spiritual growth—precious spiritual assets that will serve you a lifetime.

Examining different religions provides a universal and cross-cultural look into the ideology modern organized religion holds concerning the subject of pet death, grief for a pet, and the human-pet bond.

Contemporary Paganism

Contemporary paganism is a term used to describe practitioners of witchcraft, shamanism, revived ancient traditions, earth religions, folk magic, folk medicine, and specific occult sciences of positive intent that practice reverence for or recognition of nature. Through paganism humanity has acquired a renewed unity and appreciation with nature. Practitioners focus reverence upon the cycles of nature and observe kinship with other living creatures. Reviving the ancient human-nature bond helps to direct attention and acceptance toward the human-pet bond.

Reverence of nature coupled with increased environmental awareness offers pet owners solace, acceptance, and a new hope. Animals, just like humans, are seen as children of the earth. All of nature's cycles and life forms are harmonized and connected, bringing to light the hopeful theology of reunion through death, rebirth through reincarnation, and definitions of death and afterlife. Paganism teaches that animals are beautiful creatures that share this planet with humans and are to be respected, humanely treated, and loved. Their environments are to be preserved and their lives cherished. This component of paganism is only one of the benefits individuals receive from practicing such spiritual traditions.

At such a devastating time as pet death, pagans find the greatest compassion and understanding because they live to commune with nature.

When people first think of animals and paganism, they often conjure images of black cats, werewolves, and other traditionally associated wildlife. Sadly, many fallacies still exist, including ones that say practitioners sacrifice animals. The entire contemporary pagan community practices a love of the earth's creatures and would never think of harming them.

The pagan religion of Wicca is one of many religions whose deities are especially interested in nature's living creatures. Several animals represent the God and Goddess of Wicca. All living creatures are of the God's and Goddess' domain, and are thought of as akin to humanity, not beneath humanity or existing to be enslaved. A significant importance regarding animals is taught through Wicca. Nature is revered, symbolized by the God and Goddess who represent the male and female aspects of nature. The Goddess is the universal mother and is a symbol of eternal wisdom, fertility, and nurturing. Life is a gift She gives with the promise of rebirth at death. The Goddess is the cradle, but She is also the tomb. Therefore, most practitioners will ask Her for strength, guidance, and nurturing during their mourning and coping with a loved one's death.

As nature's seasons are symbolically demonstrated in the Wiccan Wheel of the Year, animals are held as sacred symbolic representations of the God and Goddess. All creatures are believed to have the universal life force that permits existence of life upon the physical and esoteric planes.

The Goddess has the reign of the sea, moon, stars, and the earth. All creatures, pets included, are divine in Her and the God. The cat and dog, popular family pets, are two of the numerous creatures associated with the Goddess and God.

Wicca is a beautiful religion consisting of universal harmony. As practitioners are attuned to the energy of the universe within themselves and others, their consideration of animal life is similar to that of the Unitarian-Universalist beliefs (see below). Throughout Wicca's rituals and magical workings, animals are held sacred as practiced by Native American religions. Individuals have personal animal totems, or familiars, which they often use symbolically through magical workings in circle to bring forth positive energies and qualities.

When a Wiccan who belongs to a coven experiences the tragic loss of a dear animal friend, the coven should recognize the loss in their next meeting, talk with the grieving individual, and discuss what help is needed emotionally and spiritually. Discussion should include what the individual wants or needs in order to make the arrangements desired for their pet—be it formal burial, home burial, or cremation. If the coven member so desires, a ritual can be planned. The Crossing the Bridge ritual (as described in Chapter 6) can be conducted at the time of burial or with the ashes upon cremation. The coven can decide whether or not to arrange a circle in which magic may be done to assist the beloved's passing soul as it ascends to divinity with the God and Goddess.

A solitary Wiccan usually has access to fellow practitioners through a network. I strongly suggest the solitary

Wiccan seek out the compassion and interaction with brothers and sisters of the Craft for help with internal healing.

Solitary practitioners of all pagan traditions can formulate their own Crossing the Bridge ceremony or plan their next ritual to include special phases dedicated to the passing of their beloved pet from the physical plane to the spiritual plane.

Each practitioner will cope with pet death in his or her unique fashion. You need to understand that only time can heal your grief, and under the guidance of your deity you will cope and move forward eventually. Be available should your friend, family member, or loved one need your support and someone to talk with.

Unitarian-Universalism

Similar to contemporary paganism, the Unitarian-Universalist churches are gaining popularity. A far cry from Christianity and other orthodox religions, the Unitarian-Universalist Association teaches as its first principle that each individual has the freedom to decide what is true for himself or herself, and act according to those beliefs. This in itself relieves any worry an individual might have that they are somehow going against their religious doctrines in grieving for a pet.

Dignity and the inherent worth of each person is part of the interdependent web of existence, which is the second principle. When a Unitarian-Universalist suffers the grief of a pet death, both principles can offer guidance.

As humans and animals are a part of this web of existence, they are bound together through love and companionship. Pets are considered very important companions to
the human life. We as humans display our true selves when
a pet calls for our attention, or when we engage with a pet.
Pets are seen as beneficial and the human-pet bond as a real
loving relationship.

The loss a pet owner feels is considered real and significant because a strand of the webbing of existence has been
broken. Guided by inherent worth and dignity, the bereaved
must be attended to by the congregation. The mourning
individual knows what the loss means to him or her, which
is different in every case; this realization is the starting point
of resolution. Other members of the congregation acknowledge the reality of the loss, show compassion, and help in
relieving the person's emptiness. Ways to mourn in a
healthy manner are discussed and demonstrated. Sharing
the grief that the death of a beloved pet brings is encouraged. These exercises are considered positive actions toward
resolution and growth.

The Unitarian-Universalist church is based in the spirit of earth-centered religious traditions, very much like the
concepts of Wicca. Animals are brothers and sisters to the
human race. St. Francis of Assisi, the Catholic saint, is
respected and often used as a role model for discussion in
the church teachings concerning animals.

Buddhism

In the teachings and philosophy of Mahayana Buddhism, the practitioner's goal is to lead all sentient beings to Supreme Freedom. The irreversible state of Supreme Bliss frees all suffering and the causes of suffering. The desire of the practitioner to reach this state is known as "the altruistic thought of bodhicitta." The statement indicates the entrance of the individual upon the spiritual path of development through Mahayana Buddhism.

An individual arrives at the altruistic thought by meditating on equanimity. The practitioner meditates and develops equanimity on what is believed fact, which is that all sentient beings have been our mother.

Mahayana Buddhism believes that all sentient beings have had countless rebirths and therefore experience a perpetuation of a previous moment of consciousness. Through this teaching the practitioner considers all sentient beings as having been mothers, including animals, and in their roles they have showed us, as individuals, great kindness. In our life, we may not recognize them as our previous mothers. We each have been reborn into new life forms. They have been our mothers many, many times and will continue to be.

Tibetan Buddhists believe that because all sentient beings, including our domestic pets, are kind to us outside of the role of mother, they deserve kindness in return and the best care to keep them happy and healthy.

Traditionally in Tibet, individuals would purchase animals that were to be butchered and keep them as domestic pets. When a person was ill, this traditional act was considered most helpful. Saving the life of an animal would bring great healing and kindness to the individual.

Holy shrines and temples in Tibet frequently were crowded with individuals walking their animals, which Buddhists believe is beneficial. An animal that sees a religious image and hears the sound of prayers or teachings will obtain a favorable rebirth.

Every day, Buddhists read aloud prayers for their domestic pets and other animals to hear. The names of the Bodhisattas and Buddhas are recited to a dying domestic pet or animal, and it is thought to be especially helpful at the time of their death. When the animal has died, holy people are requested to come and pray for the deceased. The bereaved owner can also go into the temple to pray for the animal and make offerings.

All sentient beings, regardless of whether human or animal, are believed to eventually attain the state of Supreme Freedom: Buddhahood. Because their consciousness is separable from the defilements that presently prevent their attainment of Supreme Freedom, it is possible.

Buddhists understand the grief a person feels when their pet dies. They do not recommend remaining in sadness, but rather to take positive action. Buddhists often suggest conducting religious practices, saying prayers, and casting wishes to benefit the animal's cycle of rebirths and spiritual development.

Hinduism

Ancient Hindu sages marveled at the perpetual recurrence of life (for example, the butterfly egg that grew into a caterpillar, and the caterpillar that became a butterfly). The sages reasoned that individual portions of life must be reborn through a constant cycle. This portion of life passed from vegetation to animal, animal to humankind, from one human body to another, up and down the scale of life forms. A pure and changing spirit exists beyond the impermanent material world. It is the unseen source of all individual life and all things.

Hinduism is a fellowship of all who accept and practice the law of right and diligently, sincerely seek for the truth. Hinduism has numerous deities, all of which are absorbed within the belief of one supreme God, Brahman. The goal of Hinduism is to achieve union with the eternal spirit called Brahman. Through ritual, purity, self-control, nonviolence, truth, charity, and compassion toward all living creatures, the union with God is made possible. In more ancient Hindu thought, the universal soul exists in each created creature of life.

The Hindus see God in everything; all life is revered. Nonviolence to animals is practiced and most Hindus are vegetarians. Cows are especially revered, for they have supplied the Hindus with milk and labor for centuries. To consume beef is a sacrilege. It is typical to observe a Hindu bowing to all cows he or she passes or witness wealthy people opening hostels to house decrepit and elderly cows. Cows wander freely through most Indian cities. Feeding the cows small offerings of food is considered a religious act.

Animals have always held a sacred position in Hinduism. Snakes are partly divine and have a god of their own. Monkeys continue to live in temples honoring Hanuman, the monkey god. Hindus like animals to celebrate sacred holidays with them. On the holiday of Dewali, elephants are painted and participate in the celebration.

The Hindu belief system offers much for the bereaved pet owner. There is sympathy and compassion for those who mourn the death of a beloved pet. The Hindus believe in reincarnation for all living creatures. Every living creature who dies goes to a purgatory, heaven, or hell—depending upon the creature's karma in life—and is then reborn. The new form of life in rebirth depends upon what the spirit did in past lives. It is believed that a better rebirth for ancestors and loved ones can be achieved by conducting special rites and pilgrimages.

Ritual, prayer, and positive action are recommended to the bereaved. Many Hindus believe in reunion with a loved one at death; they meditate on this belief to help cope with their grief.

Native American Beliefs

To best understand the Native American viewpoint, we will examine the Lakota beliefs.

In the Lakota's sacred language and beliefs, the Lakota treat nonhuman species of life as if they are human. Each species of the animal kingdom is appointed with their own nation (for example, the Owl Nation). Relationships exist between human and animal nations; companion relationships between animal nations exist as well.

The Lakota see a continuous relationship between nature and culture. They believe that as the last arrivals to the created earth, humans must strive to learn as much as the preceding life forms. As the last arrivals, humans are considered the newest, youngest, and most ignorant of life forms in the world. The medicine man/woman obtains knowledge from animals and other animate and inanimate forms that serve as advisors or helpers.

Animals and birds exhibit human characteristics and humans exhibit characteristics of other creatures. Once a medicine man/woman receives a vision, he or she may be required to act out the vision publicly and may imitate animals and birds from whom the power was derived. Humans and all animate creatures and inanimate objects are interdependent. Therefore, humans are merely another part of the universe, not greater or less than any other life form.

To the Lakota, all animate beings are born, die, and are reborn in what we understand as reincarnation.

Animals, birds, insects, trees, flowers, rocks—all living species are considered on the same level as humans. All have a soul. In English, the Lakota are often called *animists* because of this belief. The Lakota do not have a general name for the soul. Their beliefs can be described as a process consisting of four states of individualism. William K. Powers, author of *Sacred Language: The Nature of Supernatural Discourse in Lakota* (Norman, OK: University of Oklahoma Press, 1986), attributes the process to the analogy of producing fire (this analogy is Powers and is not a Lakota concept). The chart below simplifies the understanding of this process.

Analogy	Lakota Name	Definition
spark	*sicun*	Potential for being
tinder	*tun*	Transforming this potentiality through birth into an essence that is independent of the body
flame	*ni*	Providing continuous evidence that this essence exists
smoke	*nagi*	Providing evidence that the essence, independent of the corporeal existence, continues after death

The Lakota believe in these four states as four aspects of a soul. At death, the soul is free of its potentiality to be reborn into another organism (that is, reincarnation). All Native Americans believe death is a natural cycle of life. Death is not to be feared.

Pet death is understood and accepted as a reality. As with the death of a human loved one, ritual activities and prayer are recommended to assist the departed soul toward reincarnation. Although grief is felt, energies are focused on ritualistically assisting the soul beyond and preserving the deceased loved one's memory. Communication with ancestors and deceased loved ones is possible. Death does not mean the end to a loving relationship, but rather a transformation.

Judeo-Christianity

One disturbing factor for grieving pet owners is that the scriptures of the Christian faith suggest that only humans have a soul (although the scriptures do not deny that animals have souls as well).

The Bible's New Testament does not contain the word "pet" anywhere in its text.[2] References are made to animals in general, discussing the utilitarian functions animals served in human's survival and that animals should be treated humanely. We know through writings from ages ago that farm animals and those that performed utilitarian roles often shared shelter with their human owner. The ideology of people having companion animals did not exist at the time when the Bible was written. The human-pet bond was a thing of the future.

Due to these facts, many individuals who practice Christianity become frustrated when no criteria discusses the souls or value of animals or pet loss. In our modern society, some Christian spiritual leaders have genuine concern and are facing the subject.

In pet bereavement books written by authors who are of the Christian religion, almost all mention other belief systems in order to provide insight. References are made to Native Americans and Eastern philosophies. Many Christian authors of pet bereavement recommend that readers seek out and ingest the writings of transcendental poets for their beautiful compassion and hope. These authors also suggested that readers examine metaphysical philosophers who emphasize teachings similar to Eastern religions and reverence to nature.

Jesus Christ's death and resurrection emphasizes that new life is born of death. In the Old Testament, reincarnation was a consideration. Resurrection means a new life born into heaven or union with God. You might consider that your pet's soul will resurrect in heaven and that eventually you will reunite. You might also look at the loss of your pet as an opportunity to love once again, symbolic of rebirth.

Judeo-Christian theology is based on a God of love who has created all life lovingly. Genesis, the first book of the Bible, mentions that human beings are to be caretakers to the other creatures of God. They are to sustain loving relationships with all of the creatures. Like God, they are to treat all life with the utmost love.

The biblical story of Noah and the ark best describes the Christian viewpoint about animals. That story describes God's covenant as made to all living creatures—not merely human beings. In many Christian denominations, leaders are trying to establish a better understanding of God's consideration for the human-pet bond by extracting biblical references and applying them. This is also done to help pet owners who need counseling for pet bereavement.

Within the scriptures, God grieves for all he created when it is no longer physically alive. Therefore, it is natural for Christians to grieve their pets.

If you are a Christian seeking comfort for a pet's loss, read the Bible and find all the references that describe how God feels about animals. Schedule a private time when you can read alone and use a pen and paper to note the references. Take the parts you have recorded and forget their specific meaning in the Bible for a moment. Interpret them from within your own personal spiritual beliefs. The Bible will act as a tool in this exercise as you gain a better understanding of how your faith considers the human-pet bond and the value of animal life.

Concerning euthanasia, Christianity's scriptures define mercy killing to prevent suffering and terminal pain as an expression of God's love. This can be ascertained by reading the Bible. The act of mercy killing is considered to bestow a personal blessing, although the act is disturbing, and an emotionally painful and personal one.

Every Christian denomination takes sections of the Bible and applies them differently. Your beliefs reside deep within and can help to interpret scriptures in a beneficial way. Use your discretion and be true to yourself.

Catholicism

St. Francis of Assisi, one of the Catholic saints, loved all of God's creation and devoted himself to God. He felt that humans were harmonized with God, other living creatures, and the whole of nature. During your grief, read about the life of St. Francis; he was a man who lived and felt as you do.

Judaism

Judaism, like Christianity, practices a deep concern for the humane treatment of animals but has no doctrines concerning the human-pet bond. Judaism views all living creatures as God's creation; humanity has the responsibility to protect and treat them with love.

Exodus, the second book of the Bible, is an excellent source for people who need to understand how Judaism feels about animals. Exodus 20:10 and Deuteronomy 5:14 specifically apply Sabbath laws of rest to the animal kingdom and exhibits the importance of providing care to animals. The text states that animals must be kept protected and free from stress and pain, even if it means keeping two animals away from each other, should one be stronger and possibly hurt the other. Another section of interest is Numbers 23.

In Judaism, strict laws must be followed to be good and kind owners of pets and animals. Concerning the death of a pet, most sources of opinion have nearly the same attitude: there should be sympathy for the grieving pet owner and careful planning and suitable arrangements for the pet's remains. The deceased pet, having brought life and love to his or her owner, deserves loving care in death. Once the death has occurred and the proper disposal of the remains made, there is to be no further mourning or the practice of unnecessary and expensive actions to preserve the lost life. Reasonable mourning is respected, accepted, and tolerated.

Endnotes

1. Sife. *The Loss of a Pet*, p. 135.
2. Ibid., pp. 136, 137.

Afterword

DURING YOUR MOURNING, YOU MAY FEEL EMPTiness, confusion, and distress. Even after the healing and resolution, many questions will remain unanswered and a part of your grief will always exist. During the whole process, however, try to concentrate on the joyous moments you had with your pet. The love between you and your pet is eternal; consider that your reunion may come to be at your moment of crossing the threshold into the spiritual plane.

No amount of discussion or information can prepare you for the loss of a pet or make your grieving process easier. I understand that and have experienced the sadness and difficulty myself. My deepest desire and hope is that this book has made your grieving easier, given you a head start toward resolution by offering explanations of your feelings, and provided you with insight into the many factors concerning your pet's final arrangements.

May the Gods and Goddess bless you and your beloved pet. Always remember that through grief you are not alone—you are feeling the natural emotions of grief that we all share. Open your mind, look within yourself, and talk with your God or Goddess as an additional method of coping and gaining resolution. Have faith in yourself. Your love for your pet and his or her love for you will forever exist in the cosmic universe as an energy that never fades.

Appendix

Centers for Pet Bereavement Counseling

Listed below are centers where counseling about pet death is available. If none of these locations are convenient for you, write or call them to ask if they can direct you to a resource in your area. If the technology is available to you, look for information on the Internet.

The University of California
School of Veterinary Medicine
Davis, CA 95616
Call their Hotline at 1–916–752–4200

The Animal Medical Center
510 East 62nd Street
New York, NY 10021
212–838–8100
This center was featured on the Arts & Entertainment channel's TV series "Dogs," and is highly recommended.

The University of Minnesota
School of Veterinary Medicine
1635 Gortner Ave.
Minneapolis, MN 55108
612–624–6244

Glossary

Alienation—A feeling of deep disappointment that leads to withdrawal or abstinence of feelings, affections, or daily activity. Usually, alienation is an emotional response that is overcome through the process of grief. If it is not overcome in good time, the mourning individual should seek professional assistance.

Altar—Placed in the center of a cast circle or sacred space, the altar represents the cosmos, universal energies, the earth, yourself, and your spiritualism. The right side of the altar is symbolic of the God; symbols, objects, or ritual tools related to him are placed on that side. The left side is symbolic of the Goddess; symbols, objects, or ritual tools related to her are placed on that side.

Anointing Oil—An essential oil used in rituals to anoint participants in blessing, to purify, or to help in shifting consciousness.

Apathy—An absence of feeling. Through grieving, individuals may not care about anything, including themselves, and have an absence of emotion. Caution must be taken if this stage is prolonged.

Batter—To self-inflict emotional abuse by a grieving individual. To self-batter is to inflict an overwhelming emotional attack that is not physical.

Bereavement—An emotional state resulting from being deprived of a loved one.

Bond—The emotional attachment between yourself and your pet or yourself and any loved one.

Bowl of Salt—During a ritual, participants use a bowl of salt in a mixture with water to purify the cast circle or sacred space. It is symbolic of the God and placed on the right side of the altar.

Bowl of Water—During a ritual, participants use a bowl of water in a mixture with salt to purify the cast circle or sacred space. It is symbolic of the Goddess and is placed on the left side of the altar. (A cauldron of water may be substituted.)

Cauldron—An ancient vessel for cooking and brewing that is symbolic of magical and spiritual transformations; it is the sacred grail or Sea of Primeval Creation. It is also symbolic of the Goddess, immortality, the element of water, fertility, reincarnation, and inspiration. If small, the cauldron is placed on the altar's center-left. If large, it sits on the floor to the left of the altar.

Censer—A fireproof container that holds burning incense. Symbolic of the God, it is placed on the right side of the altar.

Circle—Your circle or constructed sacred space is a product of energy—a construction that can be sensed and physically felt with experience. In many pagan religions, the circle is a solid barrier that often represents the Goddess.

Columbarium—A repository at a pet cemetery for storing ashes of cremated bodies. Some cemeteries allow this unique burial option.

Cremains—The ashes of a body after the cremation procedure.

Cremation—A procedure where the deceased's body is placed on a heat-safe tray and slid into a large, oven-like structure that ignites a white-hot flame. Afterward, the remaining skeleton is ground down into ashes.

Crossing the Bridge Ritual—Practitioners of Wicca, the contemporary pagan religion, use this rite to bid farewell to deceased loved ones and assist their crossing the threshold at death into Summerland.

Cup—Has the same purpose and symbolism as the cauldron. Some pagan traditions use the cup as a drinking vessel during ritual.

Deity—A term used to generically describe "god" or "goddess." Your deity is the supreme being, creator, or source of your spiritual beliefs.

Depression—A psychological state of feeling inadequate, overwhelmingly distressed, and deeply saddened. If prolonged, professional intervention is needed.

Drinking Vessel—Any goblet, chalice, drinking horn, or drinking glass filled with a beverage for ritual consumption. The drinking vessel symbolizes the Goddess, the element of water, and fertility, and is placed on the altar's left side.

Euthanasia—The procedure of injecting drugs to induce death in a pain-free, humane fashion. Currently available to animals and prison death row inmates only.

Fantasy—The act of creating a pleasing mental image to satisfy an inner need.

Freeze-Drying—A sophisticated procedure where the deceased pet's body is held in a desired position by a supporting structure and the body artistically prepared. The body is then placed within an enormous tank for several months to internally freeze-dry. This procedure is very costly.

Humane—A compassionate, respectable, and intense attitude of consideration for other life forms.

Metamorphosis—An evolution in transition to a higher level of development or divinity.

Morbidity—As a result of disease or intense emotional upset, a state of overwhelming misery, emotional or physical discomfort, or pain.

Neurotic—Individual and personal psychological behavior resulting from insecurity, internal conflict, and internal tension.

Obsessive—Having excessive interest or repeated action in something that can evolve to an abnormal practice.

Ossuary—A vault or structure at a cemetery that contains the bones or ashes of the deceased.

Pathological—Unhealthy mental or physical action that is damaging to a person's well-being.

Post-Traumatic Stress—A condition that develops due to intense emotional shock and marked by exceptional stress.

Prognosis—Consideration of how a disease or ailment will change over a length of time.

Ritual Knife—A Wiccan ritual tool used to direct personal power and energy during ritual work. Usually it is not used for cutting or eating. Also called an athame.

Self-Defeat—Unconsciously destroying one's purposes of thought or action, inducing guilt or blame.

Self-Recrimination—Blaming oneself for actions or a lack of action that could not have been predetermined, controlled, or altered.

Sentient—A living creature who is consciously aware and who perceives and thinks.

Skyclad—A contemporary pagan term meaning naked. In theory, a participant who conducts ritual in the natural state of physical being allows for greater comfort, stands before the Gods as created without humanmade clothing, and has greater freedom of movement and shifting of consciousness in ritual.

Summerland—A contemporary pagan term describing the spiritual plane where the deceased travel. Heaven; an earth-like sanctuary.

Syndrome—A particular problem that has related symptoms typical of that problem.

Taxidermy—Artistically preparing a deceased animal body by removing the internal organs for the purpose of stuffing the body. The procedure has many sophisticated steps and includes the use of preserving chemicals. Taxidermists can also remove and preserve the animal's pelt (fur).

Transcendence—Excelling or surpassing usual spiritual limits.

Trauma—A physical, mental, or emotional condition of shock resulting from an intense injury or stress that can produce disordered behavior or feelings.

Unconscious—The mind's functioning that exists beyond the levels of awareness.

Vulnerable—Not defending oneself in any manner or assuming control of what happens to oneself. To be left open physically, mentally, or emotionally for possible damage.

Wand—Any tree branch or wood of any type, constructed into a wand of approximately eighteen inches for use in invocation of deities in ritual work. It is also used to direct energy, draw the sacred circle border upon the ground, and draw magical symbols in the air or elsewhere.

✦

Suggested Reading

PET BEREAVEMENT

Bernstein, Joanne. *Loss and How to Cope with It.* New York: Seabury Press, 1977. A guide for juveniles.

Bode, Janet. *Death Is Hard to Live With: Teenagers and How They Cope with Loss.* New York: Delacorte Press, 1993.

Donnelley, Nina Herrmann. *I Never Know What to Say.* New York: Ballantine Books, 1987. An excellent guide to learn how best to help a grieving friend or family member.

Fitzgerald, Helen. *The Grieving Child: A Parent's Guide.* New York: Simon & Schuster, 1992.

Holmes, Marjorie. *To Help You through the Hurting.* New York: Doubleday, 1983.

Lightner, Candy. *Giving Sorrow Words: How to Cope with Grief and Get On with Your Life*. New York: Warner Books, 1990.

Nieberg, A. Herbert, and Arlene Fischer. *Pet Loss: A Thoughtful Guide for Adults and Children*. New York: Harper & Row, 1992.

Quackenbush, Jamie, and Denise Graveline. *When Your Pet Dies: How to Cope with Your Feelings*. New York: Simon & Schuster, 1985.

Sife, Wallace. *The Loss of a Pet*. New York: Howell Book House, 1993. A reference book for this text. Excellent.

CONTEMPORARY PAGAN RELIGIOUS BOOKS

Buckland, Raymond. *Buckland's Complete Book of Witchcraft*. St. Paul, MN: Llewellyn Publications, 1986. Learn about Wiccan philosophy and ritual.

Campanelli, Pauline. *Wheel of the Year: Living the Magical Life*. St. Paul, MN: Llewellyn Publications, 1992. Learn about Wicca. Includes a section on communication with deceased loved ones during Halloween.

Clifton, Chas S. *Witchcraft Today: Book Two: Rites of Passage*. St. Paul, MN: Llewellyn Publications, 1993. Includes actual Wiccan rites pertaining to death.

Hope, Murray. *Practical Celtic Magic*. London, England: The Aquarian Press, 1987. In part, discusses a Celtic viewpoint of death in religion and mythology.

Lorler, Marie-Lu. *Shamanic Healing: With the Medicine Wheel*. Albuquerque, NM: Brotherhood of Life, 1989.

Meadows, Kenneth. *The Medicine Way: A Shamanic Path to Self-Mastery*. Rockport, MA: Element Books, 1990. Includes a Shamanic viewpoint and understanding of death.

O'Regan, Vivienne. *The Pillar of Isis*. London, England: The Aquarian Press, 1987. In part, discusses death from the Goddess aspect and contemporary pagan and ancient Egyptian viewpoints.

Robertson, Olivia. DEA: *Rites and Mysteries of the Goddess*. England: Cesara Publications, 3rd Impression, 1988.

———. *Rite of Rebirth*. England: Cesara Publications (date not available).

Schueler, Gerald and Betty. *Coming Into the Light*. St. Paul, MN: Llewellyn Publications, 1989. Rituals of Egyptian magick; focuses, in part, on meeting with deceased loved ones and understanding death through Egyptology.

Starhawk. *The Spiral Dance: A Rebirth of the Ancient Religion of the Great Goddess*. San Francisco: Harper & Row, 1979.

TECHNIQUES FOR MEDITATION, CHAKRA THERAPY, AND COPING AND HEALING

These books offer coping and healing techniques that can help with your grief and other emotional challenges in life.

Adair, Margot. *Working Inside Out: Tools for Change*. Berkeley, California: Wingbow Press, 1984.

Finley, Guy. *Freedom From the Ties That Bind: The Secret of Self-Liberation*. St. Paul, MN: Llewellyn Publications, 1994.

———. *The Secret of Letting Go*. St. Paul, MN: Llewellyn Publications, 1990.

Harner, Michael. *The Way of the Shaman*. San Francisco: Harper & Row, 1981.

Hope, Murray. *The Psychology of Healing*. Rockport, MA: Element Books, 1989.

———. *The Psychology of Ritual*. Rockport, MA: Element Books, 1988.

Humphrey, Naomi. *Meditation: The Inner Way*. London, England: The Aquarian Press, 1987.

Lautie, Raymond, and Andre Passebecq. *Aromatherapy: The Use of Plant Essences in Healing*. Wellingborough, England: Thorsons Publishers Limited, 1979.

Lemesurier, Peter. *Healing of the Gods: The Magic of Symbols and Practice of Theotherapy*. Rockport, MA: Element Books, 1988.

Rainwater, Janette. *Self-Therapy: A Guide to Becoming Your Own Therapist*. New York: Crucible Publishing Company, 1989.

Tisserand, Robert. *Aromatherapy to Tend and Heal the Body*. Wilmot, WI: Lotus Light, 1989.

✦

LOOK FOR THE CRESCENT MOON

Llewellyn publishes hundreds of books on your favorite subjects! To get these exciting books, including the ones on the following pages, check your local bookstore or order them directly from Llewellyn.

ORDER BY PHONE
- Call toll-free within the U.S. and Canada, 1-800-THE MOON
- In Minnesota, call (612) 291-1970
- We accept VISA, MasterCard, and American Express

ORDER BY MAIL
- Send the full price of your order (MN residents add 7% sales tax) in U.S. funds, plus postage & handling to:

   Llewellyn Worldwide
   P.O. Box 64383, Dept. (K or L #)
   St. Paul, MN 55164–0383, U.S.A.

POSTAGE & HANDLING
(For the U.S., Canada, and Mexico)
- $4.00 for orders $15.00 and under
- $5.00 for orders over $15.00
- No charge for orders over $100.00

We ship UPS in the continental United States. We ship standard mail to P.O. boxes. Orders shipped to Alaska, Hawaii, The Virgin Islands, and Puerto Rico are sent first-class mail. Orders shipped to Canada and Mexico are sent surface mail.

International orders: Airmail—add freight equal to price of each book to the total price of order, plus $5.00 for each non-book item (audio tapes, etc.).

Surface mail—Add $1.00 per item.

Allow 4–6 weeks for delivery on all orders.
Postage and handling rates subject to change.

DISCOUNTS
We offer a 20% discount to group leaders or agents. You must order a minimum of 5 copies of the same book to get our special quantity price.

FREE CATALOG

Get a free copy of our color catalog, *New Worlds of Mind and Spirit*. Subscribe for just $10.00 in the United States and Canada ($30.00 overseas, airmail). Many bookstores carry *New Worlds*—ask for it!

Visit our website at www.llewellyn.com for more information.

ANIMAL-SPEAK
The Spiritual & Magical Powers of Creatures Great & Small

Ted Andrews

The animal world has much to teach us. Some animals are experts at survival and adaptation, some never get cancer, some embody strength and courage while others exude playfulness. Animals remind us of the potential we can unfold, but before we can learn from them, we must first be able to speak with them.

In this book, myth and fact are combined in a manner that will teach you how to speak and understand the language of the animals in your life. *Animal-Speak* helps you meet and work with animals as totems and spirits—by learning the language of their behaviors within the physical world. It provides techniques for reading signs and omens in nature so you can open to higher perceptions and even prophecy. It reveals the hidden, mythical and realistic roles of 45 animals, 60 birds, 8 insects, and 6 reptiles.

Animals will become a part of you, revealing to you the majesty and divine in all life. They will restore your childlike wonder of the world and strengthen your belief in magic, dreams, and possibilities.

0–87542–028–1, 400 pp., 7 x 10, illus., photos, softcover   **$17.95**

JOURNEY OF SOULS
Case Studies of Life Between Lives

Michael Newton, Ph.D.

This remarkable book uncovers— for the first time—the mystery of life in the spirit world after death on earth. Dr. Michael Newton, a hypnotherapist in private practice, has developed his own hypnosis technique to reach his subjects' hidden memories of the hereafter. The narrative is woven as a progressive travel log around the accounts of 29 people who were placed in a state of superconsciousness. While in deep hypnosis, these subjects describe what has happened to them between their former reincarnations on earth. They reveal graphic details about how it feels to die, who meets us right after death, what the spirit world is really like, where we go and what we do as souls, and why we choose to come back in certain bodies.

After reading *Journey of Souls*, you will acquire a better understanding of the immortality of the human soul. Plus, you will meet day-to-day personal challenges with a greater sense of purpose as you begin to understand the reasons behind events in your own life.

1–56718–485–5, 288 pp., 6 x 9, softcover $12.95

PSYCHIC PETS & SPIRIT ANIMALS
True Stories from the Files of FATE Magazine

FATE Magazine Editorial Staff

In spite of all our scientific knowledge about animals, important questions remain about the nature of animal intelligence. Now, personal testimony compels us to raise deeper questions. Are some animals, like some people, psychic? If human beings survive death, do animals? Do bonds exist between people and animals that are beyond our ability to comprehend?

Psychic Pets & Spirit Animals is a varied collection from the past 50 years of the real-life experiences of ordinary people with creatures great and small. You will encounter psychic pets, ghost animals, animal omens, extraordinary human-animal bonds, pet survival after death, phantom protectors, and the weird creatures of cryptozoology. Dogs, cats, birds, horses, wolves, grizzly bears—even insects—are the heroes of shockingly true reports that illustrate just how little we know about the animals we think we know best.

The true stories in *Psychic Pets & Spirit Animals* suggest that animals are, in many ways, more like us than we think—and that they, too, can step into the strange and unknown realm of the paranormal, where all things are possible.

1–56718–299–2, 272 pp., mass market, softcover $4.99

THE JOY OF HEALTH
A Doctor's Guide to Nutrition and Alternative Medicine

Zoltan P. Rona M.D., Sc.

Finally, a medical doctor objectively explores the benefits and pitfalls of alternative health care, based on exceptional nutritional scholarship, long clinical practice, and wide-ranging interactions with "established" and alternative practitioners throughout North America.

The Joy of Health isa must-read before you seek the advice of an alternative health care provider. Can a chiropractor or naturopath help your condition? What are viable alternatives to standard cancer care? Is Candida a real disease? Can you really extend your life with megavitamins? Might hidden food allergies be the root of many physical and emotional problems?

- Get clear-cut answers to the most commonly asked questions about nutrition and preventive medicine
- Explore various treatments for 47 conditions and diseases
- Make informed choices about diets and supplements
- Discover startling information about food allergies and related conditions
- Explore 20 different types of diets and recipes
- Cut through advertising claims and vested-interest scare tactics
- Empower yourself to achieve a high level of wellness

0–87542–684–0, 264 pp., 6 x 9, softcover   **$12.95**

ENTERING THE SUMMERLAND
Customs and Rituals of Transition into the Afterlife

Edain McCoy

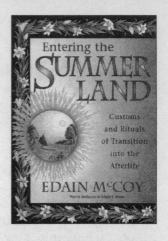

All of us must face it sooner or later—the devastating loss of a loved one. For Pagans, the period of mourning can be especially trying, simply because many are isolated from a community which shares their spiritual viewpoint of death and the afterlife. Unlike the mainstream religions, paganism has had no written guide specifically designed to offer comfort and direction to the bereaved—until now. *Entering the Summerland* fills this need by providing rituals for healing and passing, as well as practical ideas about dealing with grief. *Entering the Summerland* builds concepts and ideas about death into a framework for open discussion, ritual structure, funeral planning, and bereavement support. It also attempts to legitimize griefs that are not yet acceptable to the larger society in which we live, such as mourning the loss of a pet or a familiar.

1–56718–665–3, 256 pp., 7 x 10, illus., softcover $17.95

DREAMS & WHAT THEY MEAN TO YOU

Migene González-Wippler

Migene González-Wippler

Everyone dreams. Yet dreams are rarely taken seriously—they seem to be only a bizarre series of amusing or disturbing images that the mind creates for no particular purpose. Yet dreams, through a language of their own, contain essential information about ourselves which, if properly analyzed and understood, can change our lives. In this fascinating and well-written book, the author gives you all of the information needed to begin interpreting—even creating—your own dreams.

Dreams & What They Mean to You begins by exploring the nature of the human mind and consciousness, then discusses the results of the most recent scientific research on sleep and dreams. The author analyzes different types of dreams: telepathic, nightmares, sexual, and prophetic. In addition, there is an extensive Dream Dictionary, which lists the meanings for a wide variety of dream images.

Most importantly, González-Wippler tells you how to practice creative dreaming—consciously controlling dreams as you sleep. Once a person learns to control his dreams, his horizons will expand and his chances of success will increase!

0–87542–288–8, 240 pp., mass market   **$4.99**

A RICH MAN'S SECRET
An Amazing Formula for Success

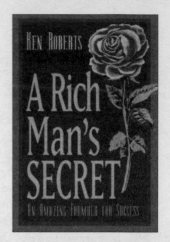

A Novel by Ken Roberts

Victor Truman is a modern-day Everyman who spends his days scanning the want ads, hoping somehow to find his "right place." He has spent years reading self-help books, sitting through "get rich quick" seminars, living on unemployment checks, practicing meditation regimens, swallowing megavitamins, listening to talk radio psychologists ... each new attempt at self-fulfillment leaving him more impoverished in spirit and wallet than he was before.

But one day, while he's retrieving an errant golf ball, Victor stumbles upon a forgotten woodland cemetery and a gravestone with the cryptic message, "Take the first step—no more, no less—and the next will be revealed." When Victor turns sleuth and discovers that this stone marks the grave of wealthy industrialist Clement Watt, whose aim was to help spiritual "orphans" find their "right place," he is compelled to follow a trail of clues that Mr. Watt seems to have left for him.

This saga crackles with the excitement of a detective story, inspires with its down-home wisdom and challenges the status quo through a penetrating look at the human comedy that Victor Truman—like all of us—is trying to understand.

1–56718–580–0, 208 pp., 5¼ x 8, softcover $9.95

TRUE HAUNTINGS
Spirits with a Purpose

Hazel M. Denning, Ph.D.

Do spirits feel and think? Does death automatically promote them to a paradise—or as some believe, a hell? Real-life ghost-buster Dr. Hazel M. Denning reveals the answers through case histories of the friendly and hostile earthbound spirits she has encountered. Learn the reasons spirits remain entrapped in the vibrational force field of the earth: fear of going to the other side, desire to protect surviving loved ones, and revenge. Dr. Denning also shares fascinating case histories involving spirit possession, psychic attack, mediumship and spirit guides. Find out why spirits haunt us in *True Hauntings*, the only book of its kind written from the perspective of the spirits themselves.

1–56718–218–6, 240 pp., 6 x 9, softcover $12.95

THE ULTIMATE CURE
The Healing Energy Within You

Dr. Jim Dreaver

The Ultimate Cure will open a door into consciousness and literally bring you into a direct, first-hand experience of illumination—an experience that will stimulate your mind, warm your heart, and feed your soul.

Dr. Jim Dreaver provides a firsthand account of the spiritual journey and outlines the steps needed to live in the world with an authentic sense of wisdom, love, and power. He addresses the issues of meditation, work as a spiritual exercise, harnessing the power of the mind, conscious breathing, and healing the wounds of the past. Dr. Dreaver's main theme is that spiritual presence, which is the source of all healing, is an actual, palpable reality that can be felt and tapped into.

To realize enlightenment, you must have a tremendous hunger for it. This delightfully honest and wonderfully human book will stimulate your appetite and, by the time you turn to the last page, will leave you feeling totally satisfied.

1–56718–244–5, 288 pp., 6 x 9, softcover $14.95

SOUL HEALING

Dr. Bruce Goldberg

George: overcame lung cancer and a life of smoking through hypnotic programming.

Mary: tripled her immune system's response to AIDS with the help of age progression.

Now you, too, can learn to raise the vibrational rate of your soul (or subconscious mind) to stimulate your body's own natural healing processes. Explore several natural approaches to healing that include past life regression and future life progression, hypnotherapy, soulmates, angelic healing, near-death experiences, shamanic healing, acupuncture, meditation, yoga, and the new physics.

The miracle of healing comes from within. After reading Soul Healing, you will never view your life and the universe in the same way again.

1-56718-317-4, 304 pp., 6 x 9, softcover $14.95

WHAT YOUR DREAMS CAN TEACH YOU

Alex Lukeman

Dreams are honest and do not lie. They have much to teach us, but the lessons are often difficult to understand. Confusion comes not from the dream but from the outer mind's attempt to understand it.

What Your Dreams Can Teach You is a workbook of self-discovery, with a systematic and proven approach to the understanding of dreams. It does not contain lists of meanings for dream symbols. Only you, the dreamer, can discover what the images in your dreams mean for you. The book does contain step-by-step information that can lead you to success with your dreams, success that will bear fruit in your waking hours. Learn to tap into the aspect of yourself that truly knows how to interpret dreams, the inner energy of understanding called the "Dreamer Within." This aspect of your consciousness will lead you to an accurate understanding of your dreams and even assist you with interpreting dreams of others.

0–87542–475–9, 288 pp., 6 x 9, softcover $14.95

THE SECRET OF LETTING GO

Guy Finley

Whether you need to let go of a painful heartache, a destructive habit, a frightening worry, or a nagging discontent, *The Secret of Letting Go* shows you how to call upon your own hidden powers and how they can take you through and beyond any challenge or problem. This book reveals the secret source of a brand-new kind of inner strength.

In the light of your new and higher self-understanding, emotional difficulties such as loneliness, fear, anxiety, and frustration fade into nothingness as you happily discover they never really existed in the first place.

With a foreword by Desi Arnaz, Jr., and introduction by Dr. Jesse Freeland, *The Secret of Letting Go* is a pleasing balance of questions and answers, illustrative examples, truth tales, and stimulating dialogues that allow the reader to share in the exciting discoveries that lead up to lasting self-liberation.

This is a book for the discriminating, intelligent, and sensitive reader who is looking for real answers.

0–87542–223–3, 240 pp., 5¼ x 8, softcover $9.95

THE SECRET WAY OF WONDER
Insights from the Silence

Guy Finley
Introduction by Desi Arnaz, Jr.

Discover an inner world of wisdom and make miracles happen!
Here is a simple yet deeply effec-
tive system of illuminating and
eliminating the problems of inner mental and emotional life.

The Secret Way of Wonder is an interactive spiritual workbook, offering guided practice for self-study. It is about
awakening the power of wonder in yourself. A series of 60
"Wonders" (meditations on a variety of subjects: "The
Wonder of Change," "The Wonder of Attachments," etc.)
will stir you in an indescribable manner. This is a bold and
bright new kind of book that gently leads us on a journey of
Spiritual Alchemy where the journey itself is the destination...and the destination is our need to be spiritually whole
men and women.

Most of all, you will find out through self-investigation that
we live in a friendly, intelligent and living universe that we
can reach into and that can reach us.

0–87542–221–7, 192 pp., 5¼ x 8, softcover $9.95

AN INVITATION TO DREAM
Tap the Resources of Inner Wisdom

Ana Lora Garrard
Illus. by Ana Lora Garrard

Reclaim the vibrant, creative part of yourself that dreams! Dreamwork allows you to open secret doors within yourself that only you can know. Many of us don't remember our dreams or we find them strange, chaotic, and distant from our understanding. *An Invitation to Dream* helps you discover for yourself the deeply personal messages within your dream images. Rather than giving worn-out "dictionary definitions," this book embraces the magic of dreams and honors the integrity of the dreamer.

This is a simple, clear, and inspiring dream book—one that teaches you how to listen to the wisdom offered in your dreams so that you can place yourself on your own path of awakening, renewal, and joy. You will learn how to recall your dreams more clearly, and you will learn innovative exercises for dream exploration that incorporate movement, artwork, writing, meditation, and verbal sharing. It also includes answers to basic questions about dreams, and outlines the story of the author's own dream journey. The author's colorful artwork provides a strong, visual presentation that will speak to the limitless dimension of your own creativity.

0-87542-253-5, 272 pp., 6 x 9, illus., color plates, softcover $12.95

DESIGNING YOUR OWN DESTINY
The Power to Shape Your Future

Guy Finley

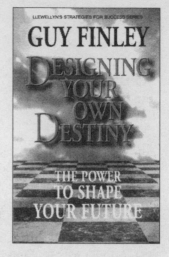

This book is for those who are ready for a book on self-transformation with principles that actually work. *Designing Your Own Destiny* is a practical, powerful guide that tells you, in plain language, exactly what you need to do to fundamentally change yourself and your life for the better, permanently.

Eleven powerful inner life exercises will show you how to master the strong and subtle forces that actually determine your life choices and your destiny. You'll discover why so many of your daily choices up to this point have been made by default, and how embracing the truth about yourself will banish your self-defeating behaviors forever. Everything you need for spiritual success is revealed in this book. Guy Finley reveals and removes many would-be roadblocks to your inner transformation, telling you how to dismiss fear, cancel self-wrecking resentment, stop secret self-sabotage and stop blaming others for the way you feel.

After reading *Designing Your Own Destiny*, you'll understand why you are perfectly equal to every task you set for yourself, and that you truly can change your life for the better!

1–56718–278–X, 160 pp., mass market, softcover $6.99